VOLUME 15 NUMBER 2 2009

Intersex and After

Edited by Iain Morland

INTRODUCTION:
LESSONS FROM THE OCTOPUS

Iain Morland

The paternalistic surgery-centered model of intersex treatment has been incisively critiqued in recent years. Feminist and antihomophobic analyses have shown how traditional medical protocols privilege male genitalia and heterosexual relationships, in particular through the assumption that penis-vagina penetration within the context of heterosexual marriage is proof positive of a successful surgical outcome. And queer analyses have begun to show that the dichotomous ossification of a patient's gender identity — another clinical goal — is both unrealistic and politically objectionable. First-person testimonies by patient advocates have largely substantiated these critiques of medical practice. There seems, then, to be a clear narrative of contestation and subsequent change emerging in the treatment of intersex. In other words, we have learned "lessons from the intersexed," as Suzanne Kessler puts it, initially about genders and gonads, but subsequently about the meaning of ethical patient care.[1]

Yet, the history of intersex treatment, which now includes the recent history of its ethical critique, is marked by a curiously disjointed temporality. If there is a lesson to be learned from the intersexed, it is structured by multiple deferrals: the deferred revelation of the outcome of David Reimer's medical management, on which much intersex treatment has been based; the now seemingly self-evident barbarity of surgical procedures that for years appeared reasonable to many clinicians and parents; the difficulties of choosing treatments, even with informed consent, that will have effects at once long-lasting and unpredictable; the inherent latency in follow-up studies of clinical outcomes, with or without surgery; the dilemma of surgical improvement whereby progress for future patients requires the use of experimental techniques on patients in the present; the stubborn asynchrony between cultural change in gender politics (and sexual politics) and con-

GLQ 15:2
DOI 10.1215/10642684-2008-133
© 2009 by Duke University Press

servative tradition in medicine; and increasingly the time lag between, on the one hand, changes in medical nomenclature and policy and, on the other, the reform of medical practice apparently expedited by new terminology and protocols. In these and other ways, I argue that the most acute "lesson from the intersexed" is that intersex treatment in the present should always be considered, paradoxically, in the light of what may come after it. Hence this special issue's title, "Intersex and After."

Accordingly, the essays published here don't constitute a manifesto for what comes after intersex; rather, they engage with the peculiar "afterwardsness" of intersex and its many lessons.[2] What happens to feminism after intersex? What happens to intersex after the shift in terminology from intersex to "Disorders of Sex Development" (DSDs)? What happens to clinical practice after multidisciplinary challenges to childhood genital surgery? What happens to the determination of sex and gender after intersex? What happens to the intersex body after surgery, and what might queer theory do about it? What happens to the meaning of ethics in intersex treatment, in the light of other types of body modification? These are some of the key questions considered by the authors of this special issue.

The first essay is "Progress and Politics in the Intersex Rights Movement: Feminist Theory in Action," by Alice D. Dreger and April Herndon, authors with experience not just of the scholarly analysis of intersex treatment but also of strategic interventions into clinical practice through patient advocacy. Their work with the influential Intersex Society of North America to change medical protocols has been substantial. Dreger and Herndon draw on this range of experience in their essay, documenting the difficult but determined rise of intersex patient advocacy in the United States during the 1990s and examining its connections to the academy, particularly feminist studies, as well as to other kinds of activism, particularly LGBT rights. While there are continuities between intersex issues and issues of gender and sexuality, Dreger and Herndon caution that there are nevertheless significant discontinuities. To this end the authors discuss their involvement in the 2005 formulation of patient-centered standards of care for what have now (by some) been termed DSDs, in an effort to focus clinical attention on those aspects of intersex that, unlike gender and sexual identities, benefit from medical care.

The relation between nomenclature, bodies, and identities is investigated in greater detail in a provocative essay by Ellen K. Feder, "Imperatives of Normality: From 'Intersex' to 'Disorders of Sex Development.'" Feder takes a longer view of the DSD terminology than Dreger and Herndon, with the aim of understanding why intersex ever seemed to be a type of identity, rather than a type of anatomy, in the first place. Building on Michel Foucault's famous analysis of the nineteenth-century emergence of sexual identities, Feder argues that the historical associa-tion (or even conflation) of intersex and homosexuality has unhelpfully implied that intersex is a disorder like no other, for it marks a kind of person—whether the "pseudohermaphrodite" of medical diagnosis or the "hermaphrodite with atti-tude" of activism. Feder makes the further suggestion that just as clinicians have disciplined intersex bodies by the use of sex assignment surgery and hormonal treatments, so too may discourse be used to discipline clinicians into managing intersex differently.

The roundtable "Intersex Practice, Theory, and Activism" is notable for its participants' wide range of backgrounds: the gynecologist Sarah M. Creigh-ton, the law professor Julie A. Greenberg, the social scientist Katrina Roen, and the visual artist Del LaGrace Volcano. Roen facilitates the discussion, in which participants tackle some of the clinical, legal, ethical, and cultural dilemmas sur-rounding intersex. Their thoughtful conversation reveals how it is not simply the case that sex and gender are constituted differently in different situations—as gender and sexuality studies have amply shown—but that what counts *as* a dilemma is inseparable from the material conditions under which sex and gender assignments are made. Such conditions include the power of the law to structure interactions between clinicians and families; the coexistence of lay and expert discourses about genital normality; and the cultural circulation of representations of sexual dissidence.

The images by Volcano that follow the roundtable, gathered here under the darkly humorous title "The Herm Portfolio," perform multiple tasks. Selected from photographic work over a fourteen-year period, they exemplify Volcano's artistic practice as discussed in the roundtable. The images illustrate Volcano's project of making critical interventions into mainstream representations of not only sex, gender, and sexuality but also class and ethnicity. Most interestingly, the images demonstrate the material constitution of dilemmas over sex and gender assign-ments: the placement together of these photographs prompts viewers to query the sexes and genders of all the photographic subjects, even in images that in circum-stances other than a *GLQ* intersex issue might not raise dilemmas at all. Taking the concealment and revelation of bodily differences as their theme, these images ask, who has the authority to conceal and reveal differences? And, what must such differences be, if they can be either concealed or revealed?

The question of whether cultural changes in the meaning and perception of bodily sex would be enough to prompt reform in the medical treatment of intersex remains unresolved by the roundtable and images. This question is addressed by Vernon A. Rosario. His contribution to the issue, "Quantum Sex: Intersex and the

Molecular Deconstruction of Sex," argues cogently for the redundancy of not only binary conceptions of sexual difference but also all deterministic accounts of sex differentiation. Drawing on recent scientific research that is often overlooked in medical and academic accounts alike, Rosario proposes that sex emerges probabilistically from a quantum cloud of biological and environmental processes, rather than being determined mechanistically by biology and environment in any given combination. This insight has practical implications for the genetic counseling of families and intersex patients, as well as for the meaning of clinical sex assignment and its long-term evaluation.

Of course, molecular biology is not the only discourse that can be used to challenge medical protocols, especially those relating to genital surgery for intersex. For *GLQ*'s readership, queer theory may also be useful. The question that my own essay therefore asks is, what can queer theory do for intersex? If Dreger and Herndon are correct that scholars in feminist and gender studies have sometimes overlooked the pressing issues of stigma, consent, and disclosure for people affected by intersex, in favor of celebrating the multigender or gender-free possibilities that intersex apparently exemplifies, then it is important to evaluate whether queer theory enables a better critique of medicine. Specifically I explore how queer theory might account for postsurgical bodies of diminished genital tactility. I contend that for this purpose queer theory must do more than focus on bodily sensations such as pleasure, shame, and touching.

Lastly, Nikki Sullivan's review essay, "The Somatechnics of Intersexuality," critically appraises three multidisciplinary anthologies in which the traditional medical management of intersex is, in turn, evaluated and often contested. Sullivan takes the arguments made in the anthologies—specifically those about ethical decision making—as the starting point for reconsidering how embodiment is the ground of ethics. Sullivan uses the idea of somatechnologies to indicate how original unmodified bodies do not precede the technological modification of some unusual bodies; instead, all bodies are constituted within a technological field that at once enables and constrains their sensibilities, including the capacity for ethical judgment. Consequently, Sullivan argues that one's embodied cultural location crucially makes certain somatechnologies intelligible as body modification in the first place, prior to any conscious judgment about whether such modifications are right or wrong. This challenges us to think about the embodiment of all agents in the intersex treatment controversy, not just patients. Doctors and parents have bodies, too.

To readers of *GLQ*, the medical management of intersex may now seem "constituted by the very incomprehensibility of its occurrence," as Cathy Caruth has written of trauma.[3] But as the essays in this special issue make clear, it is not without concrete determinants; indeed, these determinants are often the most effective grounds on which treatment can be critiqued. Correspondingly, although it might appear very odd that infant genital surgery—sometimes accompanied by gender reassignment and almost always accompanied by secrecy—became the standard Western treatment for intersex in the 1950s and has persisted almost until today, I don't think this happened because clinicians and families of people born with intersex anatomies have been mad or evil, as some might claim (and I write as one who has suffered from the negative effects of multiple surgeries). There are two contributory factors to the surprisingly uncontested uptake of the treatment model that I'd like to offer, in closing, alongside the explanations discussed elsewhere in this special issue.[4] While analyses of the treatment model's influence in terms of the histories of gender, sex, and sexuality are astute, they ought to be considered in relation to other intellectual and scientific contexts that at first glance seem less relevant to the medical management of intersex.[5]

The first factor is the intersex treatment pioneer John Money's imaginative combination of classical psychoanalytic determinism and ego psychology. In the former, certain genitals must be in place, and be seen, in order for psychosexual differentiation to occur; in the latter, clinical treatment can ameliorate conflict between self and body, and in turn between individual and society. This combination produced an invidious slippage between a concern for exterior physical genitalia and the resolution of interior psychological conflict—as if the modification of infant genitalia were itself a preemptive therapeutic practice. The second factor is mid-twentieth-century scientific humanism (of which ego psychology became a part, I'd argue), which optimistically figured the "plasticity" of gender, ethnicity, and educability as an essential part of being human. The surgical assignment of gender therefore seemed to exemplify human nature, precisely because it taught the lesson that humans have no nature in particular. In these ways (and doubtless several others), the traditional treatment model straddles multiple understandings of selfhood in Western culture—a potent mix enabling the model to work as an "ideological octopus," which has appealed for many years to traditionalists and progressives alike.[6]

Future research on intersex should continue to interrogate the multidisciplinary contexts in which its medical management has emerged, octopus-like. For if such contexts have made medical protocols obdurate, they have also left intersex treatment open to critique from multiple disciplines—not just gender and sexuality studies—all with lessons to teach the octopus.

Notes

I wish to thank the *GLQ* editors and anonymous reviewers for their generous assistance, and the contributors for their expertise, diligence, and patience. I am grateful also for Peter Hegarty's stimulating comments on a draft of this introduction.

1. Formative works in the ethical criticism of intersex treatment include Cheryl Chase, letter to the editor, *Sciences*, July–August 1993, 3; Milton Diamond, "Pediatric Management of Ambiguous and Traumatized Genitalia," *Journal of Urology* 162 (1999): 1021–28; Milton Diamond and H. Keith Sigmundson, "Sex Reassignment at Birth: A Long Term Review and Clinical Implications," *Archives of Pediatric and Adolescent Medicine* 150 (1997): 298–304; Alice Domurat Dreger, *Hermaphrodites and the Medical Invention of Sex* (Cambridge, MA: Harvard University Press, 1998); Dreger, ed., *Intersex in the Age of Ethics* (Hagerstown, MD: University Publishing Group, 1999); Anne Fausto-Sterling, "The Five Sexes: Why Male and Female Are Not Enough," *Sciences*, March–April 1993, 20–25; Fausto-Sterling, *Sexing the Body: Gender Politics and the Construction of Sexuality* (New York: Basic, 2000); Suzanne J. Kessler, "The Medical Construction of Gender: Case Management of Intersexed Infants," *Signs* 16 (1990): 3–26; and Kessler, *Lessons from the Intersexed* (New Brunswick, NJ: Rutgers University Press, 1998). For a fuller discussion of feminist and queer analyses of medical practice, see the essays in this special issue by Alice Dreger and April Herndon ("Progress and Politics in the Intersex Rights Movement: Feminist Theory in Action"), and by me ("What Can Queer Theory Do for Intersex?").
2. The term *afterwardsness* comes from Jean Laplanche. See his "Notes on Afterwardsness," in *Jean Laplanche: Seduction, Translation, and the Drives*, ed. John Fletcher and Martin Stanton (London: Institute of Contemporary Arts, 1992), 217–23.
3. Cathy Caruth, introduction to "Psychoanalysis, Culture, Trauma II," ed. Caruth, special issue, *American Imago* 48 (1991): 419.
4. I have discussed these factors in greater depth in "Thinking with the Phallus," *Psychologist* 17 (2004): 448–50; and "Plastic Man: Intersex, Humanism, and the Reimer Case," *Subject Matters* 3–4 (2007): 81–98.
5. The role of what Bernice L. Hausman has called "the idea of gender" in the development of intersex treatment is contentious (*Changing Sex: Transsexualism, Technology, and the Idea of Gender* [Durham, NC: Duke University Press, 1995]). On the one hand, it seems clear that John Money significantly interiorized gender as something not of the body. One effect of this was to make the successful surgical assignment of gender measurable by criteria other than technical quality; postsurgical genitalia of even the most dubious appearance could be valued by Money not so much for their resemblance to "natural" genitals but for their production of alleged psychosexual normality in the form of a patient's stable gender identity. This applies to both intersex and transex surgeries. (For more on the meaning of postsurgical "normality," see

my "The Injustice of Intersex: Feminist Science Studies and the Writing of a Wrong," in *Toward a Critique of Guilt: Perspectives from Law and the Humanities*, ed. Matthew Anderson [New York: Elsevier, 2005], 60–62; and Ellen K. Feder, this issue.) On the other hand, to say that gender was interiorized in Money's psychiatric discourse is to risk suggesting that gender was or is *only* interiorized and *only* a construct of psychiatry. Vernon Rosario has fiercely challenged Hausman on this point in his review of her book (*Configurations* 4 [1996]: 243–46), and Jay Prosser's *Second Skins: The Body Narratives of Transsexuality* (New York: Columbia University Press, 1998) offers an important account of gendered embodiment that does not ascribe so much discursive power to clinicians. My aim in the context of this introduction is not to resolve the highly complex question of how gender functioned in Money's work but simply to indicate that its function is contested and benefits from consideration in relation to other historical developments.

6.   I'm indebted for this phrase to Justin Lewis, *The Ideological Octopus: An Exploration of Television and Its Audience* (New York: Routledge, 1991).

PROGRESS AND POLITICS IN THE INTERSEX RIGHTS MOVEMENT

Feminist Theory in Action

Alice D. Dreger and April M. Herndon

Since 1990, when Suzanne Kessler published her groundbreaking feminist analysis of the understanding of gender among clinicians treating children with intersex, many academic feminists have produced important scholarly work on intersex and intersex rights.[1] A notable few have also lent their energies to actively working for intersex rights in medical and mainstream social arenas. Although the intersex rights movement and feminist scholarship on intersex have both progressed considerably since 1990, there remains theoretical and political irresolution on certain key issues, most notably those involving intersex identity and the constitution of gender.

This essay considers the progress made in intersex rights since 1990 and delineates important points of contention within feminist intersex scholarship and intersex politics. We argue that in the last fifteen years much progress has been made in improving medical and social attitudes toward people with intersex, but that significant work remains to be done to ensure that children born with sex anomalies will be treated in a way that privileges their long-term well-being over societal norms. We also argue that, while feminist scholars have been critically important in developing the theoretical underpinnings of the intersex rights movement and sometimes in carrying out the day-to-day political work of that movement, there have been intellectual and political problems with some feminists' approaches to intersex.

The authors have a foot in both camps considered here — academic feminism and intersex rights work. We are academic feminists who also worked

GLQ 15:2

DOI 10.1215/10642684-2008-134

as paid directors at the Intersex Society of North America (ISNA), the longest-running, best-funded, and historically most influential intersex advocacy group. Alice Dreger began working with ISNA in 1996 and volunteered as chair of its board of directors from 1998 to 2003 and 2004 to 2005, and as chair of the fund-raising committee in the 2003–4 interim. In 2005 she left the board to take on the paid, part-time position of director of medical education, which she completed in late 2005. April Herndon was employed full-time as director of programming for ISNA from June 2005 to May 2006, producing and updating educational and Web site materials, organizing speakers and volunteers, writing grants, and so forth. Dreger's graduate training is in the history and philosophy of science; in academic practice she is an historian of medicine and a bioethicist. Herndon's graduate training is in American studies; in academic practice she is a women's studies and cultural studies scholar.

A word on terminology is in order here. In this essay we use the term *intersex* to refer to variations in congenital sex anatomy that are considered atypical for females or males. The definition of *intersex* is thus context specific. What counts as an intersex phallus, for example, depends on local standards for penises and clitorises. Similarly, as we elaborate below, a person with no obvious sex ambiguity but with "sex chromosomes" other than simply XX (female-typical) or XY (male-typical) is today considered an intersex person by some intersex advocates, medical researchers, and clinicians, but not by all.[2] Yet such a person could not have been considered intersex before the ability to diagnose "sex chromosomes." So the definition of intersex depends on the state of scientific knowledge as well as general cultural beliefs about sex.

For this reason, in practice we define a person as intersex if she or he was born with a body that someone decided isn't typical for males or females. (This is also ISNA's current definition — not a coincidence, since Dreger helped develop this definition at an ISNA board retreat around 2000.)[3] Delineating intersex ultimately depends on delineating males and females, and when you get into the nitty-gritty of biology, this is not a simple task; nature is messy and often surprising, as Vernon Rosario argues in this volume.[4] That said, there are some forms of intersex that make a person's body obviously different from what is usual — for example, when a child is born otherwise male but without a penis, or when a child is born otherwise female but with a very small vagina and a large clitoris. So when we say that intersex is context specific, we do not mean to imply that these biological variations are not real but that how many variations (and thus people) are included in the category intersex depends on time and place.

Several dozen known biological variations and conditions may be considered intersex. Some have their basis in genetic variations. Some result from nongenetically caused prenatal developmental anomalies. A few involve "ambiguous" genitalia, but not all do; some involve more subtle blends of female and male types — for example, when a person has the external appearance of one sex but internally most of the organs of the other sex. Making things rather confusing to the novice, the medical names for various intersex conditions may refer specifically to the genotype (genetic basis), or to the phenotype (body type), or to the etiology (causal pathway of the condition), or to some combination of these. So saying someone is "intersex" does not tell you anything specific about a person's genes, anatomy, physiology, developmental history, or psychology. *Intersex* functions as a blanket term for many different biological possibilities — and as we show, many different political possibilities too.

Background History of Intersex

Historical records in the West suggest that until well into the twentieth century intersex people tended simply to blend in with the general population, living their lives as unremarkable boys, girls, men, and women. Given that notable genital ambiguity shows up once in about every two thousand births, if genital ambiguity had been considered terribly disturbing throughout Western history, there would likely exist significantly more records of legal, religious, and medical reactions.[5] Indeed, although largely ignored by medical practitioners who treat intersex today, there is in fact a body of medical literature from the nineteenth and twentieth centuries that shows that people with "ambiguous" sex anatomies lived relatively uneventful lives psychologically and socially.[6] The only reason many of these people even show up in that medical literature is that they wandered into the medical systems for some other concern, and then the physician noted their sex anomalies. Doctors often seem to have been more concerned with sex anomalies than many of their patients.

Historically the tendency in the West — in legal, medical, and religious affairs — has been to try to keep people sorted into clear male and female roles, and people with intersex seem to have generally participated in that binary sorting.[7] Lorraine Daston and Katherine Park found that in early modern France people labeled hermaphrodites were strictly required to adhere to one gender (male or female) and to partner only with someone of the other gender, to avoid the appearance of homosexual or other "deviant" sexuality.[8] Dreger, Christine Matta, and Elizabeth Reis have shown that a similar system took hold in European and American medicine by the late nineteenth century.[9] The growing specter of homosexuality — *behavioral* sexual ambiguity—drove many late-nineteenth-century physicians to insist that *physical* ambiguity—hermaphroditism—must be illusory and solvable through careful diagnosis of "true" sex. Matta, for example, shows "the connection between physicians' increased interest in preventing 'abnormal' sexual behavior and their insistence that interventionist surgeries were the most appropriate means of treating cases of hermaphroditism."[10] Reis meanwhile notes that "nineteenth century doctors insisted on certainty rather than ambiguity in gender designation. . . . Choosing an infrangible sex (despite indefinite and contradictory markers) was mandatory."[11]

By the mid-nineteenth century, some surgeons began offering "corrective" operations for large clitorises, short vaginas, and hypospadias (wherein the urinary meatus—the "pee hole"—appears somewhere other than the tip of the penis). Occasionally such operations were requested by patients or by parents of intersex children.[12] But surgical "normalization" did not become the standard of care for intersex children until the 1950s, when the psychologists John Money, Joan Hampson, John Hampson, and their colleagues at Johns Hopkins University developed what came to be known as the "optimum gender of rearing" model, which held that *all* sexually ambiguous children should—indeed *must*—be made into unambiguous-looking boys or girls to ensure unambiguous gender identities.[13]

The optimum gender of rearing (OGR) model was based on the assumption that children are born psychosexually neutral at birth—that gender is primarily a product of nurture (upbringing), not nature (genes and prenatal hormones)—and that having a sex anatomy that appeared to match one's gender identity is necessary to a stable gender identity. Money and the Hampsons believed that children could be steered one way or the other so long as the steering began before the age of two, give or take a few months.[14] After the 1950s, surgeons at Hopkins and then at other major U.S. medical centers operated early to make children's genitals more closely approximate the typical genitals of the gender assigned. They also removed gonads that did not match the assigned gender, even if those gonads were healthy and potentially fertile. When the child reached the age of puberty, endocrinologists administered hormones to push secondary-sex development in the direction of assigned gender if the hormones produced by the child's own endocrine glands were inadequate to the task. Most children were assigned female because of the belief that it was easier to make a convincing-looking girl than a convincing-looking boy. (At least one surgeon has summed it up, "You can make a hole but you can't build a pole.")[15] Boys were expected to have reasonably sized and reasonably functional penises; girls were primarily expected to be able to be on the receiving end of penile penetration.[16]

The team at Hopkins also provided intensive psychological gender coaching, though this last aspect of treatment was less common at other medical centers, even while everyone agreed intersex represented a psychosocial concern.[17] Although defenders of the Hopkins OGR team point out that their publications include suggestions that intersex children be told their medical histories in age-appropriate ways, in practice and in print many clinicians favored deception and withholding of medical records, lest patients become confused and depressed by their intersex states.[18] By the early 1990s it was common practice for medical students and residents to be taught that their ethical duty meant deceiving women born with XY chromosomes and testes, telling them, if anything, that they had "twisted ovaries" that had to be removed.[19] The pediatric endocrinologist Jorge Daaboul remembers telling women with XY chromosomes that they had one regular X chromosome and one X chromosome with a short arm, something he knew a Y chromosome is not.[20]

History of the Intersex Rights Movement

Kessler's 1990 *Signs* article, the first publication to provide a sustained feminist critique of the OGR model, explored the sexist and heterosexist assumptions made by clinicians working with intersex patients regarding what counts as normal for girls and boys.[21] Using published medical literature as well as original interviews with intersex clinicians, Kessler demonstrated that the medical treatment of intersex was directed primarily at obscuring, and when possible eliminating, apparent sex and gender ambiguity.

Anne Fausto-Sterling brought a feminist understanding of intersex to a wider audience in 1993 by simultaneously publishing "The Five Sexes" in *The Sciences* and an op-ed called "How Many Sexes Are There?" in the *New York Times*.[22] In these companion pieces Fausto-Sterling reiterated and thus publicized the existing medical taxonomy of five sex types, a division that had coalesced in the late nineteenth century.[23] These included males, females, true hermaphrodites (which Fausto-Sterling called "herms"), male pseudohermaphrodites ("merms"), and female pseudohermaphrodites ("ferms"). "Herms" were people with both ovarian and testicular tissues; "merms" were people with ambiguous or mixed-sex anatomy and testes; "ferms" were people with ambiguous or mixed sex anatomy and ovaries. Fausto-Sterling's purpose was to challenge the pervasive belief that sex (and thus, in many people's minds, gender) came in a simple dichotomy.

In response to Fausto-Sterling's article Cheryl Chase (now known as Bo Laurent) published a letter in *Sciences* announcing the formation of ISNA.[24] Cognizant of how people with intersex were treated as if they were shameful and in need of strict social discipline, Chase originally planned to call the organization "Intersex Is Not Criminal."[25] Around the time of Fausto-Sterling's articles, Chase and other intersex people, including Max Beck, Morgan Holmes, and Kiira Triea, had come to the realization that they had been wronged by the medical establishment and that they needed to agitate for the rights of children born like them.[26] Because intersex activists felt the harm that had come to them had occurred largely because of the medicalization and medical mismanagement of intersex, they focused their attentions on critiquing the OGR model. In doing so, these activists were informed by principles of feminism (particularly the right to speak for oneself and critiques of sexism), gay and lesbian rights (particularly critiques of heterosexism and homophobia), and patients' rights (especially regarding autonomy, informed consent, and truth telling).[27]

Slowly at first (from about 1993 to 1999) and more rapidly later, intersex activists found allies in academic feminism, medicine, law, and the media. Like the activists born intersex, the great majority of nonintersex allies focused their attentions on the contemporary medical standard of care for intersex. Among the problems noted with the OGR model were these: it treated children in a sexist, asymmetrical way, valuing aggressiveness and sexual potency for boys and passiveness and reproductive/sexual-receptive potential for girls; it presumed that homosexuality (apparent same-sex relations) and transgenderism (changing or blurring gender identities) constituted bad outcomes; it violated principles of informed consent by failing to tell decision-making parents about the poor evidentiary support for the approach; it violated the axioms of truth telling and "first, do no harm"; it forced children to have their bodies adapted to oppressive social norms, using surgeries and hormone treatments that sometimes resulted in irrevocable harm; it generally involved treating psychosocial issues without the active participation of psychosocial professionals such as psychologists, psychiatrists, and social workers.[28] A more recent critique questions whether there is any reason to believe nonstandard genitals constitute a psychological risk factor; in fact, the medical literature fails to support the medical establishment's foundational assumption that having intersex genitals significantly increases psychosocial risk.[29]

As intersex advocacy grew so did the number and prominence of activist and support organizations for people born with intersex. Partly to make up for the gap left by ISNA's move away from day-to-day support toward systematic medical reform, the Internet-based, U.S.-located Coalition for Intersex Support, Activism, and Education (CISAE), founded by Triea and Heike Boedeker, and Bodies Like Ours, founded by Janet Green and Betsy Driver, sought to provide active peer support for parents and affected adults. Emi Koyama conceived Intersex Initiative as a relatively local group, originally focused on Portland, Oregon, but she has since brought it to national prominence. Diagnosis-specific groups such as the international Androgen Insensitivity Syndrome Support Group (AISSG) thrived throughout the late 1990s and continue today. However, not all relevant patient advocacy groups agreed with ISNA, Bodies Like Ours, and Intersex Initiative that the OGR model had to go: for example, the CARES Foundation (for congenital adrenal hyperplasia) and the MAGIC Foundation (for conditions that affect children's growth, including some types of intersex), run mostly by parents and clinicians, tended to remain in agreement with the medical establishment.

Independent of advocacy organizations, some sex researchers and clinicians took a stand against the OGR, most notably Milton Diamond and his associates. Diamond and H. Keith Sigmundson reported what happened to David Reimer, the nonintersex boy whose transformation into a girl (following a circumcision accident) Money had directed.[30] Money had claimed Reimer's gender transformation worked—and that therefore the OGR system was likely to work for intersex children. But Money was lying; Money knew Reimer had not been happy as a girl, and indeed transitioned socially to a boy almost as soon as he learned of his past.[31] Knowing this and hearing the painful stories of many adults with intersex, Diamond called in 1998 for a moratorium on intersex genital surgeries while data was collected on outcomes.[32]

Initially the medical establishment mostly ignored critiques and calls for change, issuing only occasionally a restatement of the belief that the OGR model was necessary and effective.[33] These statements rarely answered the specific critiques noted above. When Dreger edited a 1998 special issue on intersex for the *Journal of Clinical Ethics* (which became the basis for the 1999 anthology *Intersex in the Age of Ethics*), she tried to find a clinician who would defend the OGR model, but could not. Notably, several were by that point willing to criticize it.[34] The one critique to which traditionalist clinicians did begin to respond was the lack of outcomes data in favor of the approach. The outcomes data that has recently emerged is mixed and tends to vary wildly in terms of implicit assumptions on the goal of intersex treatment.[35]

Since about 2004, there has been a marked increase in interest among clinicians to reform practice. For example, thanks to the initiative of the feminist academic sociologist Monica Casper, who served as ISNA's executive director in 2003, ISNA developed a medical advisory board of approximately twenty-five people, most of them clinicians, something that seemed a distant dream as late as 1998. In 2004, at the American Academy of Pediatrics Section on Urology meeting, many clinicians were clearly agonizing over the choice of treatment in intersex cases. Even surgeons who had historically been ardent defenders of the OGR model were publicly expressing serious reservations.[36] In October 2005 the highly influential Lawson Wilkins Pediatric Endocrine Society and the European Society for Paediatric Endocrinology held a consensus meeting in Chicago that resulted in a hopeful degree of movement toward providing more psychosocial care, peer support, truth telling, informed consent, and outcomes data.[37]

Also in 2005, a collective comprised mostly of the three stakeholder groups—intersex people, parents of intersex people, and clinicians—formed and issued new clinical guidelines and a handbook for parents based on a "patient-centered model of care," an explicit alternative to the OGR.[38] That group, known as the Consortium on the Management of Disorders of Sex Development (or DSD Consortium for short), was formed as a result of grants given to ISNA to complete, produce, and distribute drafts written several years earlier by the social workers Sallie Foley and Christine Feick. The DSD Consortium includes founders and leaders of many of the major diagnosis-specific intersex support groups as well as clinicians from all the specialties involved in intersex care. (We were members of the DSD Consortium, and Dreger led the project as coordinator and editor in chief.)

The DSD Consortium's *Clinical Guidelines* state:

> Patient-centered care means remaining clearly focused on the well-being of individual patients. In the case of DSDs this specifically involves the following principles.
>
> 1. Provide *medical and surgical care when dealing with a complication that represents a real and present threat.* . . .
>
> 2. Recognize that what is normal for one individual may not be what is normal for others. . . .
>
> 3. Minimize the potential for the patient and family to feel ashamed, stigmatized, or overly obsessed with genital appearance; avoid the use of stigmatizing terminology (like "pseudo-hermaphroditism") and medical photography; *promote openness.* . . .
>
> 4. Delay elective surgical and hormonal treatments *until the patient can actively participate in decision-making.* . . .
>
> 5. *Respect parents by addressing their concerns and distress empathetically,* honestly, and directly. . . .
>
> 6. *Directly address the child's psychosocial distress* (if any) with the efforts of psychosocial professionals and peer support.
>
> 7. Always *tell the truth* to the family and the child.[39]

These principles may seem like common sense, but they are considered somewhat radical by clinicians who have long believed that the presence in a child of a trait that challenges social norms means the most basic tenets of medical ethics can (and indeed must) be set aside.[40]

The DSD Consortium's handbooks are drawing much interest and praise in medical centers around the United States and are being distributed by advocacy groups (such as the MAGIC Foundation) historically supportive of the medical establishment. Our own experience suggests that clinicians who until recently practiced the OGR model are quite receptive to the patient-centered alternative. We see this as clear evidence that the changes for which intersex activists first hoped in the early 1990s are finally happening. This is not to overlook continued delays in the implementation of a reformed model. In our experience many medical centers currently lack institutional resources—including adequately trained psychosocial professionals, leadership, cross-disciplinary relationships, and funding—needed to implement psychosocially attentive integrated team care. Some also suffer from disputes among clinicians over the best approach. But more and more are expressing interest in providing something like the patient-centered, multidisciplinary team approach recommended by the DSD Consortium.[41]

The success of the intersex rights movement is almost certainly due in part to concomitant success in the LGBT rights movement. As noted above, the treatment of intersex has historically been motivated by homophobia and transphobia—that is, fear of apparent same-sex relations and fear of people changing or blurring gender categories. Positive changes in social attitudes toward queer-identified people have thus led to positive changes in social attitudes toward people with what some have called "queer bodies."[42] Success can also be credited to the fact that intersex advocates have been extremely effective at using the power of the media to change minds.[43] Substantial Western media attention to intersex people and intersex medicine, as well as the publication in 2002 of Jeffrey Eugenides's Pulitzer Prize–winning *Middlesex: A Novel*, has helped make the existence of intersex known, believed, and understood by tens of millions more people. We should note that, although a few intersex people objected to Eugenides's portrayal of an intersex person because it was a fictional story by a nonintersex man, our experience has been that the learning engendered by his novel for doctors and laypeople alike has been generally progressive. (Both of us have been surprised at how many conservative older men and women have told us excitedly what they learned about intersex from reading *Middlesex* in book clubs, including Oprah Winfrey's.) The intersex rights movement has also benefited from several talented writers—including Martha Coventry, Esther Marguerite Morris Leidolf, and

Triea—who have conveyed their personal histories with eloquence and power.[44] We see therefore many reasons to believe that the intersex rights movement will continue to make marked progress in the coming years, even while we are concerned that the skyrocketing marketing of genital cosmetic procedures—including penile enlargement and labia reduction surgeries—has the potential to produce a negative effect on intersex clinical reform, as norms for genital appearance become increasingly visible and rigid.[45]

Intersex Identity Politics

Although people sometimes refer to "the intersex community" as they do "the lesbian community," this is somewhat misleading. There are online virtual communities of people with intersex, but large numbers of intersex people do not live together in brick-and-mortar communities, and only occasionally do they come together for meetings that are primarily about political consciousness-raising rather than about sharing information about particular medical diagnoses (like hypospadias or congenital adrenal hyperplasia). ISNA has hosted a few small invitation-only retreats, and a number of intersex people have come together at the annual Creating Change conference of America's National Gay and Lesbian Task Force, and for one-time events such as the 2002 "Rated XXXY" San Francisco fund-raiser produced by the intersex advocate, performer, and poet Thea Hillman, but such gatherings remain either irregular or infrequent.

There are sizable annual meetings of diagnosis-specific groups like the AISSG, the CARES Foundation, and the Hypospadias and Epispadias Association, but often the participants of these meetings do not consider themselves "intersex" and are in fact offended by the term being used in reference to them. Objections we have heard include that the term sexualizes them (or their children if the objector is a parent) by making the issue one of eroticism instead of biology; that it implies they have no clear sex or gender identity; and that it forces on them an identity, especially a queer identity, to which they do not relate.[46]

Historically the word *intersex* as we know it dates to the early twentieth century when it was coined by the biologist Richard Goldschmidt as a term for biological sex types that fell between male and female.[47] Throughout the twentieth century, members of the medical profession occasionally used the term to refer to what they would more typically call hermaphroditisms or pseudohermaphroditisms. Early intersex advocates chose the term because it was less confusing and stigmatizing than terms based on the root *hermaphrodite*, although occasionally they used those alternate terms for in-your-face self-empowerment. For example,

ISNA's first newsletter was called *Hermaphrodites with Attitude*, and Chase's 1996 video of ten intersex people telling their own stories was called *Hermaphrodites Speak!* But today few intersex advocates call themselves "hermaphrodites" both because the irony is lost on most people and because the term makes intersex people sound like mythical figures who are simultaneously fully male and fully female—something physiologically impossible but a frequent fantasy of certain fetishists who e-mail support groups seeking "hermaphrodite" sex partners. (Such people are known contemptuously in intersex activist circles as "wannafucks.") Early in the intersex rights movement, activists, scholars, and journalists sometimes referred to *intersexuals*, but this term has largely fallen out of favor because it can be essentializing and dehumanizing to equate people with one aspect of their physicality. Instead, many advocates and activists now prefer to use terms such as *person with intersex*, *intersex person*, or *person with an intersex condition*, taking a cue from the disability rights movement.[48]

As suggested above, the question of who counts as intersex remains contentious. The people who made up the early intersex rights movement tended to share a common experience: they were born with noted sexual ambiguity, surgically "corrected" as young children, subjected to continued medicalization and stigma inside and outside the clinic, and they eventually developed a queer political consciousness that allowed them to understand their plight as unjust. But as the intersex rights movement grew, the diversity of actual experiences became more obvious, and this led to internal questions of identity politics. Were people intersex who "just" had hypospadias? Were women intersex who had well-controlled congenital adrenal hyperplasia and very little genital "masculinization" (so little it was never medically "fixed")?

The movement tended to welcome all these people out of the generosity that typically marks early social movements looking for people who will help and be helped.[49] But the anxiety about who should belong is obvious in venues like *Hermaphrodites Speak!* where Tom, born with hypospadias, jokes, "I'm the real hermaphrodite here—these people are just imposters." The intersex activist David Iris Cameron took to carrying around a card that asked, "Is XXY intersex?"[50] Cameron has Klinefelter syndrome (XXY chromosomes), which the layperson prone to a simplistic algebraic understanding of "sex chromosomes" might think of as obviously intersex. But many physicians do not count Klinefelter syndrome as intersex, just as they do not count Turner's syndrome (one X with no second "sex chromosome"), because in many physicians' minds, neither results in enough external sex-atypical development to count.

In our experience some clinicians have played a sort of moving target game whereby their definition of intersex changes from venue to venue, or moment to moment. We end up spending a remarkable amount of time just trying to agree on which diagnoses (and thus which people) count in the conversation we're trying to have. This does not usually seem to be a purposeful attempt to stall or derail conversation (although that does sometimes result); rather it seems to stem from a lack of systematic consideration of what the term might mean. For example, some want to call intersex only those born with visibly ambiguous genitalia, or only those who have had a particularly unusual mix of prenatal sex hormones.

Two illustrations: the physician William Reiner, a longtime ISNA ally, has tended to insist that males born with cloacal exstrophy are not intersex because their brains are not subjected prenatally to a sex-atypical mix of hormones.[51] Yet in cases of cloacal exstrophy, because the gut wall does not form properly, males are born with no penis. Standard practice (challenged by Reiner's work) has been to assign these children as girls, castrate them, and give them feminizing hormones starting at the age of puberty. In other words, the children are *treated* as intersex. Indeed, in all other cases when a boy is born with very little or no penis, the child would fall under the category intersex. Yet Reiner—who has been a staunch advocate of both intersex rights and the well-being of children born with cloacal exstrophy—seems not to want to apply the intersex label to cloacal exstrophy males purely because they have male-typical prenatal brain development.

A second example: in a recent discussion with a clinician, the name of one particular intersex activist came up, and the clinician stopped conversation to say, "she isn't intersex, she was just progesterone-virilized." In other words, given her genotype the activist in question would have developed as a standard female, but because her mother was given progesterone during pregnancy (presumably to prevent miscarriage), the activist's genitals had been virilized to some degree in the womb. So this activist was born with ambiguous genitalia, and as a result she was sent through the OGR system. Yet because she had medically induced (rather than "naturally" occurring) genital virilization, the clinician did not think she counted as intersex.

To make matters even more confusing, sex development is complicated enough that two people who share nominally the same condition may have quite different genotypes (genetic codes) or phenotypes (body types). For example, just knowing a person has ovotestes (misleadingly called "true hermaphroditism" in the medical literature) won't reveal much about the person's chromosomes or even his or her genitalia; a person with ovotestes may appear fairly feminine, fairly masculine, or in-between in terms of genitalia and overall physique. The majority of people with ovotestes have XX (female-typical) sex chromosomes, but others have

XY or some other combination. Moreover, genitals that start as "ambiguous" may become naturally less so, and vice versa. Sharon Preves notes the case of Sierra, a child born with a large clitoris. The doctors wanted to shorten the clitoris for psychosocial reasons. Her mother refused. Several weeks later Sierra's clitoris shrunk to a normal size.[52] She probably had genital engorgement—that is, blood had pooled in her genitals, causing them to temporarily swell, from her being squeezed through her mother's birth canal. Had Sierra had surgery she might now count as intersex. Because of her mother's good sense she now probably doesn't count by anyone's definition.

The definitional challenges encountered with physicians, combined with the rejection of the intersex label by many parents and affected adults, have led us to participate in a move toward using a new blanket term: *disorders of sex development* (DSDs). When we started working with the group that became the DSD Consortium, it became clear that we couldn't reach agreement on practice unless we came to agreement on terminology. Otherwise we couldn't say to whom our guidelines applied. Everyone recognized that it was critical to avoid all terms based on the misleading and stigmatizing "hermaphrodite."[53] Alternative available medical terms included *disorders of sex(ual) differentiation* and *disorders of sexual development*. Terms with *sexual* in them were rejected because of the implication that we were talking primarily about an issue of sexuality (eroticism, orientation) instead of sex (anatomy and physiology). "Differentiation" was rejected in favor of "development" because of disciplinary disagreement about what "differentiation" means. (Endocrinologists mean one thing, geneticists another.) One participant, David Iris Cameron, suggested "variations of sex development," but this was rejected for discounting the health concerns that come with some intersex conditions—concerns like dangerous endocrine imbalances and an increased risk of gonadal cancers. Besides, "variations" would describe every human, not just the people we meant to describe, namely, those liable to be treated as problematically sex-atypical. In the end handbook contributors settled on "disorders of sex development," with many people in the group expressing enormous relief at this.

As noted above, the DSD Consortium's handbooks represented significant progress. The consortium included past and present leaders from many other critically important advocacy and support groups, including the AISSG, the CARES Foundation, ISNA, the MRKH Organization (for girls and women born with conditions including incomplete vaginal development), and Bodies Like Ours. In other words, we achieved buy-in on a clearly articulated patient-centered model of care among people who previously appeared not to agree. We know that this would have been impossible without the shift of nomenclature to DSD.

At the same time that the DSD Consortium was working in earnest, in October 2005 the Lawson Wilkins Pediatric Endocrine Society and the European Society for Paediatric Endocrinology held their consensus conference on intersex. One agreement reached at that meeting was to abandon the terms *intersex* and *(pseudo)hermaphroditism* in favor of *disorders of sex development*, defined as "congenital conditions in which development of chromosomal, gonadal, or anatomical sex is atypical."[54] This was not a coincidence; several clinicians from the DSD Consortium (notably the pediatric urologist and geneticist Eric Vilain, the pediatric psychiatrist and urologist Reiner, and the pediatric psychologist David Sandberg) called for the change in nomenclature. But it is worth noting that their call fell on receptive ears; clinicians were ready for this change.

Reception of the new terminology has been mixed among people with intersex. Several months after publication of the DSD Consortium's handbooks, three participating intersex adults — Cameron, Esther Morris Leidolf, and Peter Trinkl — asked that a one-sentence disclaimer be added noting that, though they support the documents, they do not support the term. Several adults with intersex also objected to the term at an October 2006 conference held by ISNA and in written responses to the Chicago consensus document.[55] It is obvious from the way we write that, as scholars and activists, we still prefer the term *intersex* even while we recognize the usefulness of using *DSD* in many contexts.[56] Understandably, many people dislike having the label of disorder applied to them. Ironically, after years of trying to demedicalize intersex to some extent, the term we're now using remedicalizes it. But we have found that the terminology accords with the experience of many intersex adults and parents; it gives them a term that feels right in that it seems simultaneously to name, scientize, and isolate what it is that has happened. It therefore makes the phenomenon seem more manageable by being less potentially all-encompassing of their identities. Moreover, the shift to this terminology clearly has allowed serious progress toward patient-centered care, in part because it has allowed alliance building across support and advocacy groups, and with clinicians. For that reason we have been pragmatists about the nomenclature change. We strongly suspect that as attitudes and behaviors among clinicians improve, it will become possible and indeed necessary to revisit the nomenclature issue. Reis's recent suggestion of "Divergence of Sex Development" might turn out to be a viable compromise.[57]

A number of transgender people who were not born with any apparent sex anomalies and were not subjected to intersex medical management believe they should count as intersex because something in their brains obviously makes them feel differently than average males and females. One transgender person wrote to us that unless one believes in a mind-brain dichotomy (which we don't), obviously there is something sex-atypical in the brains of transgender people. But it is not clear that that sex-atypicality (always) represents a neurological intersex comprising a female brain in a male body, or vice versa. Some transgendered persons' brains may be different from the average in some way other than a neurological sex inversion.

For transgender adults, there are definite advantages to counting as intersex. For one, people in the United States tend to be more accepting of identities that have a definitive (or at least implied) biological basis. The current *Diagnostic and Statistical Manual of Mental Disorders* (*DSM-IV*) provides another reason for transgender people to seek the intersex label. According to the *DSM-IV*, a person with atypical gender identity can be classed as having gender identity disorder only if the person is not intersex.[58] Thus being labeled with an intersex condition means avoiding the diagnosis of a "mental disorder" and possibly easier access to legal and medical sex reassignment.

Yet many intersex advocates have rejected the idea that transgender people are necessarily intersex. For one thing they (and we) have found that a few transgender adults claim specific intersex conditions (like 5-alpha-reductase deficiency or partial androgen insensitivity syndrome) they don't actually have. But even beyond that, some intersex activists argue that transgender persons have had radically different experiences from intersex persons who have been through the OGR mill. Of course many (though by no means all) transgender people have experienced significant stigma for being gender atypical since childhood. But Chase writes that some transgender advocates inappropriately imply that intersex often results in gender transition, an inaccurate implication that "facilitates the doctors' misguided perceptions that incorrect gender assignment is the only harm of OGR, and that studies documenting low transition rates are evidence of success."[59] While there is no singular intersex experience to which a singular transgender experience can be compared, we think it is important to acknowledge the concern that intersex experiences and advocacy may become muddied, co-opted, or misguided in the conflation of transgender and intersex.[60]

Still, even though there may be differences between intersex and transgender, there are also reasons for intersex and trans activists to unite. As Leslie Feinberg notes, the divisive behavior of territory marking over identities often weakens the movement for human rights. Feinberg states emphatically that "we can never throw enough people overboard to win approval from our enemies."[61] Feinberg goes on to say that "people who don't experience common oppression *can* make history when they unite."[62] While there may be moments when intersex activists are justified in their demands that people understand the particulars of intersex and transgender, there is also reason to carefully consider whether these particulars are always important and why such lines are drawn in the first place. If the particulars of transgender and intersex are highlighted only in order to make intersex people more intelligible or acceptable, then the result might be that transgender people are made less intelligible or even pathologized. Thus intersex activists doing the work of cleaving intersex and transgender must diligently examine their motives and the possible outcomes of such work.

Finally, on the issue of intersex identity politics we might note for other scholars thinking about stepping into identity-centered activism that we have each been criticized and had our motives questioned for being nonintersex people working on intersex scholarship and activism. For example, we have both had our intentions interrogated in online forums, and Herndon has been attacked for daring to point out the similarities between what intersex people and fat people face in terms of stigma and medicalization.[63] But this has by no means been a frequent occurrence. In general, activists born intersex have welcomed our collaboration and have often acted as enthusiastic advisers to and supporters of our efforts.

Intersex and the Nature of Gender

Much scholarship in science and the humanities on intersex (including our own) has been motivated by attempts to ascertain the nature of gender. Historically, feminist intersex scholarship has aligned with other feminist theoretical scholarship in that it has taken gender to be a social construct distinct from sex (anatomy and physiology). For example, Kessler's 1990 intersex work aligned with her earlier work on gender by showing how social assumptions about what it means to be a male or a female are taught, learned, and reinforced. Dreger, Fausto-Sterling, Myra Hird, Holmes, Iain Morland, and many other feminist scholars working on intersex have similarly shown how social beliefs about gender are actively imposed on people whose bodies don't fit the simplistic assumptions that gender equals sex and that sex-gender formations come in only two flavors.[64]

Indeed, until relatively recently some feminists cited the alleged success of the OGR model as proof that gender is socially constructed.[65] But the concept of gender (as distinct from sex) as it developed in intersex clinical practice was hardly meant to be progressive. As Dreger has shown, the move in the early twentieth century to assigning a "workable" gender instead of a gender that aligned with a biological "true sex" was a conservative reaction to the unrelenting messiness of sex. Doctors dealing with intersex decided they had better resort to a system of gender assignment that would allow them to socially sort everyone into two types no matter how apparently in-between they were physically.[66] As Kessler and others have shown, the work of the Hopkins team continued in this tradition.[67] So even while Money and his allies supported the idea that gender is to a large degree socially constructed, in intersex care they maintained traditionalist, sexist, and heterosexist concepts.

Nevertheless, particularly in the early years of the intersex rights movement, many intersex people found feminist writings about the social construction of gender empowering and liberating. They could use this work to see how one particular construction had been forced on them and how their lives might have been better (and could yet be better) under different social constructions.[68] Social constructivism also gave solace to those who felt their gender identities did not fit into the simplistic male-female dichotomy promoted by Western popular culture. It was especially painful, therefore, for some intersex women (particularly women with AIS) to find their self-identities as women rejected by Germaine Greer in her book *The Whole Woman* because she insisted that "it is my considered position that femaleness is conferred by the final pair of XX chromosomes. Otherwise I don't know what it is."[69] As Morland has noted, when Greer was challenged by women with AIS and family members of girls with AIS, she was "dismissive; she then used the book's second edition not to retract the claims, but to publicly mock the AIS correspondents by referring to them too as men." Morland has persuasively argued that ironically "in trying to criticize the social construction of femaleness and intersex, Greer disenfranchised precisely those people who live at the intersection of the two categories."[70] Greer's simplistic and essentialist position seemed to represent something of a rearguard action against admitting anyone who might be a male-to-female transsexual into the ranks of real womanhood. Yet, we confess to never really understanding the intellectual balancing act performed by Greer and people like the leaders of the Michigan Womyn's Music Festival (who have tried hard to keep a "womyn born womyn only" policy of admission): they seem simultaneously to condemn and employ essentialist notions of womanhood.

In fact, neither a hard-line social constructivist nor a hard-line biological essentialist theory of gender seems supportable by the real-life experiences of people with intersex. On the one hand, if gender identity were purely a matter of social construction, it would not make sense that people with certain intersex conditions tend to revert to one particular gender identity despite monumental efforts aimed at making them the other. Consider, for example, the high percentage of males born with cloacal exstrophy, castrated and raised as girls, who declare themselves to be boys.[71] Similarly, many transgender people present gender identities in contradiction with the intensive gender training they've received — or indeed identities that confound any description in gendered terms.[72]

On the other hand, a simplistic biological explanation for gender identity also fails in the face of intersex. Not all males born with cloacal exstrophy or a micropenis and raised girls decide they are really boys or men. Of course, some who retain their female gender identities may be unaware of their medical histories or have plenty of reasons to decide to stay with the gender they were assigned. Gender transition comes at significant financial, physical, and emotional costs.

Ultimately it seems illogical to have so firm a belief in either the biological determination or social construction of gender that all of us with stable gender identities amount to either biologically programmed robots or victims of false consciousness. As Diana Fuss pointed out in *Essentially Speaking*, even hard-core constructivism amounts to an essentialism itself — in this case, actually a biological essentialism that presumes everyone is born with a blank slate for a brain where gender is concerned.[73]

Chase has argued that it is the very obsession with "the gender question" that has led to so much harm for people with intersex. According to Chase, while some people (like Money and some feminists) have used intersex to sit around debating nature versus nurture, real people with intersex have been hurt by these theories and their manifestations. Chase has therefore argued that "intersex [has been] primarily a problem of stigma and trauma, not gender."[74] Clearly, most OGR clinicians — from Money through today — have disagreed, arguing instead that "problems of gender identity development are *the core concern* in the psychosocial management of medical conditions involving ambiguous genitalia."[75] Yet a close reading of intersex autobiographical writing suggests that relatively few feel that getting the "wrong" gender assignment formed the central cause of their suffering. Indeed, this is a finding supported by outcome studies by OGR clinicians, . . . who then take this as proof that they've been on the right track all along![76] This failure to see why they're on the wrong track results from believing that "successful" gender identity means success in intersex patient care. Most intersex autobiographies support Chase's argument, showing how shame (including, but not limited to, shame about gender variation), secrecy, and medical mismanagement led to significant suffering.[77]

Nevertheless, contrary to Chase's simple formulation, clearly for a significant number of intersex people, gender — in the form of gender identity and gender role expectations — *is* a central concern in their lives. It is not uncommon for people with intersex to ponder how their gender identities and histories relate to their intersex. A few, like Mani Mitchell, feel that their intersex biology explains their feelings of being bigendered or intergendered.[78] Indeed, some have claimed that ISNA's message (that intersex is mostly about shame and trauma, not gender) fails to acknowledge their socially atypical genders. In fact, ISNA has never suggested people should not have the right to express their genders however they wish. ISNA (like the DSD Consortium, Bodies Like Ours, and all the diagnosis-specific support groups) has advocated raising all children as boys or girls, providing a best-guess gender assignment based on what can be surmised (after extensive tests) about the child's biology and future psychology, including how the parents are thinking about the child's gender. The reasoning behind this is twofold: (1) raising a child in a third or no gender is not a socially feasible way to reduce shame and stigma; (2) intersex is not a discrete biological category, so someone would always be deciding who to raise as male, female, or intersex: three categories don't solve the problem any more than two or five or ten do.

ISNA argued that gender assignment should not be reinforced with surgeries—that healthy tissue should be left in place for the patient to decide herself or himself what, if anything, to do with it. Although certain members of the medical establishment erroneously believed (and some still do believe) that ISNA advocated "raising children in a third gender," this was never the case. The cause of confusion seems to come from the fact that many clinicians can't understand what it would mean to raise a child with "ambiguous" genitalia as a boy or a girl, despite plenty of historical evidence that this has worked, no doubt because sex anomalies are largely hidden by clothing.[79]

We've been asked innumerable times why ISNA did not want to get rid of gender altogether. This question typically comes not from intersex adults but from scholars and students in gender studies. As Herndon noted while she was director of programming, ISNA privileged what is known from adults with intersex, and most adults with intersex don't have any problem with having a gender as men or women, nor do most reject the gender assignments given to them as children.[80] Many enjoy publicly "doing their gender," as Judith Butler would say.[81] This is true even for those who see themselves privately as third-gendered or ungendered. As noted above, most intersex adults agree that the problem with the medical management of intersex is not gender assignment but surgical and hormonal reinforcement of the assignment and other risky—and indeed physically and emotionally *costly*—manifestations of shame and secrecy.

A few critics have suggested that a better system than ISNA's would be more like what Feinberg, Kate Bornstein, and some other transgender activists promote. But our readings of Feinberg and Bornstein do not seem to be inconsistent with the message of ISNA—that people should ultimately be allowed to express their genders as they wish. Recounting a tense moment with a lesbian friend, Feinberg notes that many people believe that gender expression can only be oppressive. She writes of her friend, "She believes that once true equality is achieved in society humankind will be genderless. . . . If we can build a more just society, people like me will cease to exist. She assumes that I am simply a product of oppression."[82] Meanwhile, Bornstein notes that her own work is received in many different ways by members of the trans community, with some people agreeing with her and others being upset by her views. Trying to explain these disparate reactions, Bornstein writes, "Every transsexual I know went through a gender transformation for different reasons, and there are as many truthful experiences of gender as there are people who think they have a gender."[83] Thus several of the most visible leaders of the trans movement express views similar to those expressed by many intersex activists—that people's gender expressions need not be read only as oppressive and that the vast majority of people will have at least some positive investment in their gender expression.

The Future

Serious progress has been made in intersex rights in the last fifteen years, progress that we believe would have been much slower or even impossible without the philosophical and practical efforts of many academics who have devoted their energies to trying to end the oppression of intersex people. There remains much theoretical and practical work to be done in and around the intersex rights movement, and we fully expect that academic feminists will continue to be an essential part of this work. We believe there are key insights feminists interested in helping can develop from the history we have presented here. For one, feminists should seek to listen carefully to intersex people in the same way they have listened to other marginalized groups, rather than assume they know what is true or right for intersex people.[84] Additionally, they should seek to write about intersex people on their own terms rather than just appropriate intersex for talking about other issues like the social construction of gender. They may also help by doing more than theorizing—by helping with the day-to-day fund-raising and advocacy work that support the intersex rights movement. Finally, such feminist commentators should acknowledge that many intersex (and also transgender) people have suffered even more than biologically typical women from sexist and heterosexist oppression.

Notes

During the publication process of this essay, ISNA closed. Its Web site content remains available, and its assets have been transferred to a new nonprofit organization, Accord Alliance (www.accordalliance.org). We are grateful to Myra Hird, Emi Koyama, Bo Laurent, Esther Morris Leidolf, Kiira Triea, and especially Iain Morland for comments on earlier drafts of this essay.

1. Suzanne J. Kessler, "The Medical Construction of Gender: Case Management of Intersexed Infants," *Signs* 16 (1990): 3–26. For examples of subsequent work, see Alice Domurat Dreger, *Hermaphrodites and the Medical Invention of Sex* (Cambridge, MA: Harvard University Press, 1998); Dreger, ed., *Intersex in the Age of Ethics* (Hagerstown, MD: University Publishing Group, 1999); Anne Fausto-Sterling, *Sexing the Body: Gender Politics and the Construction of Sexuality* (New York: Basic, 2000); Michelle Morgan LeFay Holmes, "The Doctor Will Fix Everything: Intersexuality in Contemporary Culture" (PhD diss., Concordia University, 2000); Suzanne J. Kessler, *Lessons from the Intersexed* (New Brunswick: Rutgers University Press, 1998); Iain Morland, "Narrating Intersex: On the Ethical Critique of the Medical Management of Intersexuality, 1985–2005" (PhD diss., University of London, 2005); Sharon E. Preves, *Intersex and Identity: The Contested Self* (New Brunswick: Rutgers University Press, 2003).

2. "Sex chromosomes" is misleading; the X chromosome includes genes important to nonsex traits, and genes on chromosomes other than the X and Y are necessary for sex development. See Alice Domurat Dreger, "Sex beyond the Karyotype," in *Controversies in Science and Technology*, ed. Daniel Lee Kleinman and Jo Handelsman (New Rochelle, NY: Mary Ann Leibert, 2007), 467–78.

3. Intersex Society of North America, "What Is Intersex?" www.isna.org/faq/what_is _intersex (accessed July 29, 2008).

4. Vernon A. Rosario, "Quantum Sex: Intersex and the Molecular Deconstruction of Sex," this issue.

5. Intersex Society of North America, "How Common Is Intersex?" www.isna.org/faq/ frequency (accessed July 29, 2008).

6. Dreger, *Hermaphrodites*; Intersex Society of North America, "What Evidence Is There That You Can Grow Up Psychologically Healthy with Intersex Genitals?" www .isna.org/faq/healthy (accessed July 29, 2008); Christine Matta, "Ambiguous Bodies and Deviant Sexualities: Hermaphrodites, Homosexuality, and Surgery in the United States, 1850–1904," *Perspectives in Biology and Medicine* 48 (2005): 74–83; John Money, "Hermaphroditism: An Inquiry into the Nature of a Human Paradox" (PhD diss., Harvard University, 1952); Elizabeth Reis, "Impossible Hermaphrodites: Intersex in America, 1620–1960," *Journal of American History* 92 (2005): 411–41;

Elizabeth Reis, *Bodies in Doubt: An American History of Intersex* (Baltimore: Johns Hopkins University Press, 2009).

7. For an example of an exception, see the story of Thomas/Thomasine Hall in Reis, "Impossible Hermaphrodites."

8. Lorraine Daston and Katherine Park, "The Hermaphrodite and the Order of Nature: Sexual Ambiguity in Early Modern France," *GLQ* 1 (1995): 419–38.

9. Dreger, *Hermaphrodites*; Matta, "Ambiguous Bodies"; Reis, "Impossible Hermaphrodites."

10. Matta, "Ambiguous Bodies," 74.

11. Reis, "Impossible Hermaphrodites," 412–13.

12. Dreger, *Hermaphrodites*; Matta, "Ambiguous Bodies"; Reis, "Impossible Hermaphrodites."

13. John Money, Joan G. Hampson, and John L. Hampson, "Imprinting and the Establishment of Gender Role," *Archives of Neurology and Psychiatry* 77 (1957): 333–36.

14. Money, Hampson, and Hampson, "Imprinting and the Establishment of Gender Role."

15. Melissa Hendricks, "Is It a Boy or a Girl?" *Johns Hopkins Magazine*, November 1993, 15.

16. Alice Domurat Dreger, "'Ambiguous Sex'—or Ambivalent Medicine? Ethical Problems in the Treatment of Intersexuality," *Hastings Center Report* 28, no. 3 (1998): 24–35.

17. For examples of Hopkins's gender coaching, see John Colapinto, *As Nature Made Him: The Boy Who Was Raised as a Girl* (New York: HarperCollins: 2000); and Kiira Triea, "Power, Orgasm, and the Psychohormonal Research Unit," in Dreger, *Intersex in the Age of Ethics*, 141–44.

18. For a recommendation of disclosure, see John Money, Joan G. Hampson, and John L. Hampson, "Hermaphroditism: Recommendations Concerning Assignment of Sex, Change of Sex, and Psychological Management," *Bulletin of the Johns Hopkins Hospital* 97 (1955): 284–300. On withholding, see Dreger, "Ambiguous Sex"; and Anita Natarajan, "Medical Ethics and Truth-Telling in the Case of Androgen Insensitivity Syndrome," *Canadian Medical Association Journal* 154 (1996): 568–70.

19. Sherri Groveman, "The Hanukkah Bush: Ethical Implications in the Clinical Management of Intersex," in Dreger, *Intersex in the Age of Ethics*, 23–28.

20. Jorge Daaboul, "Does the Study of History Affect Clinical Practice? Intersex as a Case Study: The Physician's View" (paper presented at the annual meeting of the American Association for the History of Medicine, Bethesda, May 2000).

21. Kessler, "Medical Construction of Gender."

22. Anne Fausto-Sterling, "The Five Sexes: Why Male and Female Are Not Enough," *Sciences* (March–April 1993): 20–25; Fausto-Sterling, "How Many Sexes Are There?" *New York Times*, March 12, 1993.

23. Dreger, *Hermaphrodites*, 139–66.

24. Cheryl Chase, letter to the editor, *Sciences* (July–August 1993): 3.

25. Cheryl Chase, pers. comm., July 9, 2004.

26. Kiira Triea, "Learning about Transsexuality from Transsexuals," Transkids, www
.transkids.us/learning (accessed July 29, 2008).

27. Cheryl Chase, "Hermaphrodites with Attitude: Mapping the Emergence of Intersex
Political Activism," *GLQ* 4 (1998): 189–211.

28. Kessler, "Medical Construction of Gender"; Dreger, "Ambiguous Sex"; Kessler, *Lessons from the Intersexed*; *Hermaphrodites Speak!* dir. Cheryl Chase, Intersex Society
of North America, 1996; Julie Greenberg, "Legal Aspects of Gender Assignment,"
Endocrinologist 13 (2003): 277–86; Groveman, "Hanukkah Bush"; Holmes, "Doctor
Will Fix Everything."

29. Alice Domurat Dreger, "Intersex and Human Rights: The Long View," in *Ethics and
Intersex*, ed. Sharon Sytsma (Dordrecht: Springer, 2006), 73–86; Intersex Society
of North America, "What Evidence"; Peter A. Lee et al., "Consensus Statement on
Management of Intersex Disorders," *Pediatrics* 118 (2006): 814–15.

30. Milton Diamond and H. Keith Sigmundson, "Sex Reassignment at Birth: A Long
Term Review and Clinical Implications," *Archives of Pediatric and Adolescent Medicine* 150 (1997): 298–304.

31. Colapinto, *As Nature Made Him*.

32. Kenneth Kipnis and Milton Diamond, "Pediatric Ethics and the Surgical Assignment
of Sex," *Journal of Clinical Ethics* 9 (1998): 398–410.

33. Alice Domurat Dreger, "Cultural History and Social Activism: Scholarship, Identities, and the Intersex Rights Movement," in *Locating Medical History: The Stories
and Their Meaning*, ed. Frank Huisman and John Harley Warner (Baltimore: Johns
Hopkins University Press, 2004), 390–409.

34. See, for example, Justine M. Schober, "A Surgeon's Response to the Intersex Controversy," in Dreger, *Intersex in the Age of Ethics*, 161–68; Bruce E. Wilson and William G. Reiner, "Management of Intersex: A Shifting Paradigm," in Dreger, *Intersex
in the Age of Ethics*, 119–35.

35. See, for example, Dreger, "Cultural History and Social Activism"; Heino F. L. Meyer-
Bahlburg et al., "Attitudes of Adult 46,XY Intersex Persons to Clinical Management
Policies," *Journal of Urology* 171 (2004): 1615–19; Lee et al., "Consensus Statement"; Justine M. Schober, "Feminization (Surgical Aspects)," in *Pediatric Surgery
and Urology: Long-Term Outcomes*, ed. Mark D. Stringer, Keith D. Oldham, and Peter
D. E. Moriquand, 2nd ed. (Cambridge: Cambridge University Press, 2006), 595–610;
and Schober, "Surgeon's Response."

36. Alice Domurat Dreger, "Agonize—Then Cut This Way" (2004), www.isna.org/articles/
aap_urology_2004.

37. Lee et al., "Consensus Statement."

38. Consortium on the Management of Disorders of Sex Development, *Clinical Guidelines for the Management of Disorders of Sex Development in Childhood* (Rohnert Park, CA: Intersex Society of North America, 2006), and *Handbook for Parents* (Rohnert Park, CA: Intersex Society of North America, 2006). Both books can be read and downloaded from www.dsdguidelines.org.

39. Consortium, *Clinical Guidelines*, 2–3; emphases in original.

40. Dreger, "Ambiguous Sex"; Alice Domurat Dreger, *One of Us: Conjoined Twins and the Future of Normal* (Cambridge, MA: Harvard University Press, 2004).

41. See, for example, Lee et al., "Consensus Statement."

42. Morgan Holmes, "Queer Cut Bodies," in *Queer Frontiers: Millennial Geographies, Genders, and Generations*, ed. Joseph A. Boone et al. (Madison: University of Wisconsin Press, 2000), 84–110.

43. Chase, "Hermaphrodites with Attitude"; Dreger, "Cultural History and Social Activism"; Sharon E. Preves, "Out of the O.R. and into the Streets: Exploring the Impact of Intersex Media Activism," *Research in Political Sociology* 13 (2004): 179–223.

44. Martha Coventry, "Making the Cut," *Ms.*, October–November, 2000, 52–60; Esther Marguerite Morris Leidolf, "The Missing Vagina Monologue," *Sojourner* 27 (2001): 20–21, 28; Triea, "Power, Orgasm, and the Psychohormonal Research Unit."

45. Virginia Braun, "In Search of (Better) Sexual Pleasure: Female Genital 'Cosmetic' Surgery," *Sexualities* 8 (2005): 407–24.

46. April Herndon, "What Are Disorders of Sex Development?" (originally written for www.isna.org), www.alicedreger.com/herndon/DSDs (accessed June 5, 2007).

47. Elizabeth Reis, "Divergence or Disorder? The Politics of Naming Intersex," *Perspectives in Biology and Medicine* 50 (2007): 535–43.

48. Nowadays *intersex* is commonly used as both an adjective and as a noun. Previously *intersexed* had been the standard adjective.

49. Kiira Triea, pers. comm., August 31, 2006.

50. Alice Domurat Dreger, "Is XXY Intersex?" *ISNA News*, Fall 2002, 2.

51. William G. Reiner and John P. Gearhart, "Discordant Sexual Identity in Some Genetic Males with Cloacal Exstrophy Assigned to Female Sex at Birth," *New England Journal of Medicine* 350 (2004): 333–41.

52. Preves, *Intersex and Identity*, 148.

53. Alice Domurat Dreger et al., "Changing the Nomenclature/Taxonomy for Intersex: A Scientific and Clinical Rationale," *Journal of Pediatric Endocrinology and Metabolism* 18 (2005): 729–33.

54. Lee et al., "Consensus Statement."

55. Reis, "Divergence or Disorder?"

56. Herndon, "What Are Disorders?"

57. Reis, "Divergence or Disorder?"

58. For the reasoning behind this, see Heino F. L. Meyer-Bahlburg, "Intersexuality and

the Diagnosis of Gender Identity Disorder," *Archives of Sexual Behavior* 23 (1994): 21–40.

59. Cheryl Chase, pers. comm., September 7, 2006.

60. Triea, "Learning about Transsexuality"; April Herndon, "What's the Difference between Being Transgender or Transsexual and Having an Intersex Condition?" Intersex Society of North America, www.isna.org/faq/transgender (accessed July 29, 2008).

61. Leslie Feinberg, *Transgender Warriors: Making History from Joan of Arc to Dennis Rodman* (New York: Beacon, 1997), 98.

62. Feinberg, *Transgender Warriors*, 99; emphasis in original.

63. April Herndon, "Fat and Intersex?" (2005), www.isna.org/node/961. This practice has also been extended to intersex people; Iain Morland, who was born intersex, has had his motives questioned online because he has also identified himself as a researcher (pers. comm., December 31, 2006).

64. Dreger, *Hermaphrodites*; Fausto-Sterling, "Five Sexes" and *Sexing the Body*; Myra J. Hird, "Gender's Nature: Intersexuals, Transsexuals, and the 'Sex'/'Gender' Binary," *Feminist Theory* 1 (2000): 347–64; Holmes, "Doctor Will Fix Everything"; Iain Morland, "Is Intersexuality Real?" *Textual Practice* 15 (2001): 527–47.

65. Judith Butler, "Doing Justice to Someone: Sex Reassignment and Allegories of Transsexuality," *GLQ* 7 (2001): 624–25.

66. Dreger, *Hermaphrodites*.

67. See, for example, Kessler, "Medical Construction of Gender."

68. Dreger, "Cultural History and Social Activism."

69. Germaine Greer, "Greer Replies to the Father," www.medhelp.org/www/ais/debates/letters/father.htm (accessed July 29, 2008).

70. Iain Morland, "Postmodern Intersex," in *Ethics and Intersex*, ed. Sharon E. Sytsma (Dordrecht: Springer, 2006), 328.

71. Reiner and Gearhart, "Discordant Sexual Identity."

72. Kate Bornstein, *Gender Outlaw: On Men, Women, and the Rest of Us* (New York: Routledge, 1994).

73. Diana Fuss, *Essentially Speaking: Feminism, Nature, and Difference* (New York: Routledge, 1989).

74. Cheryl Chase, "What Is the Agenda of the Intersex Patient Advocacy Movement?" *Endocrinologist* 13 (2003): 240.

75. Meyer-Bahlburg, "Intersexuality," 21; emphasis added.

76. See, for example, Meyer-Bahlburg et al., "Attitudes of Adult 46,XY Intersex Persons."

77. See, for example, the narratives of people with intersex discussed in Kessler, *Lessons from the Intersexed* and Preves, *Intersex and Identity*.

78. *Yellow for Hermaphrodite: Mani's Story*, dir. John Keir, Greenstone Pictures, 2004.

79. Intersex Society of North America, "What Evidence Is There?"

80. Intersex Society of North America, "Why Doesn't ISNA Want to Eradicate Gender?" (2006), www.isna.org/faq/not_eradicating_gender.

81. Judith Butler, *Gender Trouble: Feminism and the Subversion of Identity* (New York: Routledge, 1990), 33.

82. Feinberg, *Transgender Warriors*, 83.

83. Bornstein, *Gender Outlaw*, 7–8.

84. April Herndon, ed., *Teaching Intersex Issues* (Rohnert Park, CA: Intersex Society of North America, 2006).

IMPERATIVES OF NORMALITY

From "Intersex" to "Disorders of Sex Development"

Ellen K. Feder

In May 2006 the U.S. and European endocrinological societies published a consensus statement announcing a significant change in nomenclature. No longer would nineteenth-century variations on the term *hermaphrodite*, or the more newly introduced term *intersex*, be used in a medical context to describe "congenital conditions in which development of chromosomal, gonadal, or anatomical sex is atypical"; instead the preferred term henceforth would be *disorders of sex development* (DSDs).[1] The announcement met with a certain amount of controversy, as evidenced by the letters—from some intersex activists as well as their allies—sent to the *Archives of Disease in Childhood* in the months immediately following the statement's publication. Those objecting to the new terminology focused on the description of intersex conditions as "disorders," which they described as "stigmatizing" to the individual who should be spared identification "as" a disorder.[2]

The treatment to which infants and children with intersex conditions have been subject since the 1950s is by now well known. Medical management of intersex, with its concern with removing any sexual ambiguity, has focused in short on surgical "fixes" for what might otherwise be understood in contemporary terms as social, political, or psychological matters of sexual identity.[3] In light of these practices, it would indeed seem that an effective response would be to take intersex out of the domain of medicine altogether, to "demedicalize" conditions that might otherwise count as ordinary human variations. Certainly many of those writing in response to the consensus statement rallied behind the suggestion of biologist Milton Diamond and attorney Hazel Beh, who argued for using the term *variations of sex development*.[4] But while it is easy to make the case that differences in genital appearance should be understood as matters of variation, such terminology does not permit appreciation of the genuine health challenges faced by many individuals with intersex conditions.

GLQ 15:2
DOI 10.1215/10642684-2008-135
© 2009 by Duke University Press

The change in nomenclature together with its attendant controversy raised significant questions that merit further exploration. Foremost is the question of the status of intersex with respect to the constitution of personal identity: has intersex taken on the status of an identity, or is it a condition that is merely incidental to one's person? The objections made to the change in nomenclature seem to take for granted first that there are such things as "intersexuals," which would render the characterization of the condition as a disorder offensive.[5] The second concern with the new nomenclature is related to the first — namely, that the pathologization putatively effected by the new nomenclature would constrain unduly the range of possibilities of affected individuals to understand themselves. That is, the pathologizing label would limit people's subjective possibilities by containing them within its terms. Underlying these two claims, I want to propose, is an implicit understanding of intersex(uality) as analogous with homosexuality. However well meaning, this comparison — together with its liberatory aims — is misplaced and reinforces the very conceptualization of intersex as a "disorder like no other" that it is intended to challenge.

In what follows I want to consider how the change in medical terminology could be understood as progressive. It brings the prospect (though of course not the certainty) of a shift in focus from gender and genitalia (and the emphasis on cosmetic surgery that has been figured as necessary for the living of a "normal life") to the *medical conditions* including the endocrinological and metabolic imbalances — sometimes severe and even life threatening — associated with some intersex conditions. Such attention is especially lacking in care for affected adults, who, having left the care of increasing numbers of pediatric specialists, find no physicians knowledgeable about the progression of a given condition or who will support them in establishing appropriate hormone replacement to compensate, for example, for the removal of gonads.[6]

In the first part of this essay, I examine the historical convergence of the treatment of homosexuality and intersex. I argue that the contemporary association of homosexuality with intersex risks obscuring those concerns unique to the treatment of intersex conditions and the consequences for affected individuals. The complex and persistent identification of homosexuality with intersex since the nineteenth century nevertheless requires that we reckon with this historical relation and its shaping of the motivations both for the prevailing standard of care that has been so harmful and for the organized resistance to these practices in the intersex movement. In response to the proposal for the change in nomenclature, we must confront the surprising fact that doctors and activists alike have focused on matters of gender and genitalia at the expense of the ordinary health concerns of affected individuals. Michel Foucault's understanding of the power of "normalization," I argue in the essay's second part, can help us make sense of the history of medicalization and its pernicious effects, but in addition can allow those with intersex conditions and their allies to understand the positive possibilities that the change from intersex to DSDs can bring. Rather than fight for the demedicalization of intersex conditions that indeed have consequences for individuals' health, acceptance of this change can transform the conceptualization of intersex conditions from their past treatment as "disorders like no other" to "disorders like many others." Understood in these terms, medical attention to those with atypical anatomies should be recast from a preoccupation with "normal appearance" to the concern with human flourishing that is the putative aim of medical practice.

Pathological Convergence: Homosexuality and Intersex

There is every reason to consider the treatment of homosexuality, both historical and contemporary, alongside the medical management of intersex conditions. At nearly every moment in modern medical investigation and the popular imagination alike, each has been implicated in the other. In the nineteenth century "sexual inversion" was understood as "the tendency to embody physical characteristics associated with the opposite sex," an idea that "homosexuals were in some sense constitutional hermaphrodites."[7] This close tie between hermaphroditism and homosexuality has a longer history, however. According to Foucault, it was not the mixing of sexes in individuals that was threatening in seventeenth- and eighteenth-century France but the crime of making "use of their additional sex" through homosexual behavior.[8] While the close connection between physical sex and object desire was, as Jennifer Terry notes, "eventually undermined as Freud's theories of sexuality achieved greater notoriety and influence in the scientific community," fears about homosexuality have shaped the medical management of intersex since the 1950s when the standard of care was first formulated.[9] As Anne Fausto-Sterling recounts in *Sexing the Body*, it would make sense for laypeople, and particularly parents of children with intersex conditions at midcentury, to conflate homosexuality — still understood as a "disorder of psychologic sex" — with intersex. "If," as she writes, "intersexuality blurred the distinction between male and female, then it followed that it blurred the line dividing hetero- from homosexual." But even if parents made category errors that "pioneers" of medical management such as John Money and John and Joan Hampson would not, Fausto-Sterling clarifies that heterosexual orientation nevertheless counted as a significant indicator of the success of medical management.[10] It appears that little has changed in the last sixty or so years. Projected sexual orientation continues to figure in decisions on gender assignment (and with it, surgical correction) of infants, as a recent survey of physicians revealed, and parents are encouraged in their expectations for "normal" (i.e., heterosexual) outcomes for their children.[11]

This historical connection between homosexuality and intersex does account, I think, for why resistance to the DSD nomenclature makes good sense on its face. It was, after all, the successful battle against the pathologization of homosexuality — its critical removal from the *Diagnostic and Statistical Manual of Mental Disorders* (*DSM*) — that has provided the foundation for the ongoing effort to secure social and political acceptance since the era of the "invert."[12] And certainly the intersex movement, from its inception in 1993, when Cheryl Chase announced the formation of a support group for those with intersex conditions, has made use of language and practices employed throughout the history of gay liberation and queer activism.[13] The very formation of the Intersex Society of North America was a reclamation of the medical term *intersex*; its publication of the newsletter *Hermaphrodites with Attitude* and the recording of the very first gathering of individuals with intersex conditions in the video *Hermaphrodites Speak!* evoke the rallying call for gay men and lesbians to "come out of the closets and into the streets," and bring to mind the contemporaneous activism of the 1990s practiced by groups like Queer Nation.[14]

Queer activism has provided not only a model of political activism but ready allies in demands for radical change in medical practice.[15] This alliance has been forged by means of what might be understood as a visceral sympathy that gay men and lesbians, and particularly those who have been subjected as children to various forms of "gender policing," may experience for those who are or have been objects of intersex management.[16] That shame is so central to the "normalizing practices" that commonly characterize the stigmatization of those with atypical anatomies and those with "deviant" sexual desires alike underscores why so many people with intersex conditions and queer activists would find common cause.

But while we might understand the enforcement of norms of gender (which always already entail norms of sexual desire) to shape the experience of those whose behavior and bodies defy these norms, we should take care to note the important differences between them. What sets the experience of those with atypical sexual anatomies apart from the pervasive sorts of "gender training" (from which no one is spared) are the conspicuous marks of enforcement borne by those with intersex conditions. While one could argue that we all wear the mark of gender on our bodies, such a characterization would trivialize the significant differences between the traces of the usual enforcement of gendered behavior and the literal scars borne by children submitted to surgery. This critical difference suggests a danger of identifying too closely the interests of LGBT communities with those with intersex conditions. Ignoring the points where the experience and interests of queer and intersexed diverge, we risk obscuring the unique needs of those with intersex conditions. The kinds of needs to which I here refer are those that *medicine has itself ignored or marginalized* in favor of a disproportionate, or even what appears in some cases to be a kind of hysterical, concern with gender and genitalia. These include the "ordinary" kinds of health problems associated with diverse intersex conditions, the sorts of challenges for which individuals with just about any other medical diagnosis would expect care as a matter of course.[17] These should become more salient when we consider what should be routine medical care for adults who must manage sometimes critical endocrinological imbalances from congenital adrenal hyperplasia (CAH) or hypopituitarism. Other conditions might require hormone replacement therapies as a result of the removal of gonads, or because gonads do not function at all (as is the case with some conditions), or their function is insufficient to prompt the pubertal changes that many individuals want.[18]

Where homosexuality was, as historian Jonathan Ned Katz puts it, "an invention" of the nineteenth century, and the homosexual, in Ian Hacking's terms, "a made-up person," intersex conditions resist comparable characterization as productions of history.[19] I do not dispute, of course, that the multiple histories of hermaphroditism have been, and should be, recounted. In the changing understandings of the morphology of the person whose sex does not fit easily into male or female, the putative moral consequences of these differences, and the spectrum of cultural responses to those individuals—social, medical, juridical—there are indeed many stories to be told.[20] But while some individuals with intersex conditions embrace an identity as "intersex," many, and some have suggested most, do not in fact choose to identify in this way (and conversely, many who are not born with a genetic or endocrine disorder affecting sex development *have* identified themselves as intersex).[21] It is therefore critical that we not lose sight of the fact that even as there are what might be described as cultural constructions of hermaphroditism, many intersex conditions are also at the same time conditions that benefit from, or positively require, medical intervention. In this respect the history of intersex management may be more aptly compared with the storied past of a disease such as tuberculosis, a medical condition whose "truth," as Hacking has put it, was slowly transformed by the late-nineteenth-century discovery of the "brute fact . . . that [tuberculosis] is a specific disease transmitted by microbes." This discovery—of an underlying cause of a condition that had previously been attributed to a different sort of individual or societal "ill"—changed but did not immediately displace the earlier belief that "consumption was not only a sickness, but a moral failing, caused by defects of character."[22] So while tuberculosis, unlike consumption, was understood at last to be a disease that was contagious, it was nevertheless considered in the United States "a disease of only some, not all people, essentially the immigrant and the poor, not the middle or upper classes."[23]

The comparison between intersex conditions and tuberculosis is obviously a limited one: while some intersex conditions (such as CAH or 5-alpha-reductase deficiency) can be heritable, intersex conditions are not contagious. Tuberculosis was associated with populations of people and activated government campaigns promoting public health; intersex conditions are generally considered individual matters, and secrecy—intended, according to physicians, to protect the privacy of individuals and their families—is maintained.[24] The comparison may nevertheless underscore the importance of attending to the underlying physiological conditions of a disease or disorder, even as we take account of the abundance of social meanings at work—a dimension that the comparison to homosexuality, as I have suggested, risks minimizing. Invoking the historical case of tuberculosis suggests that there is room both for robust criticism of the stigma attached to the bodies of those who contract the disease (or those understood to be "at risk") and for appreciating the importance of treating the condition. If at least for some period social stigma and medical "truth" coexisted in the case of tuberculosis, we may similarly regard intersex treatment to be in a state of transition.

The ongoing tension between treating intersex as a social problem (that has fallen to medicine to "cure") versus a medical problem (in the ordinary sense) is most starkly evinced by the fact that cosmetic genital surgeries for infants and children remain a significant component of care, and so understandably continue to occupy a central position in the controversy over treating affected children. The section on "Surgical Management" in the consensus statement reflects the equivocal position taken by medicine toward those with intersex conditions. While surgery may be necessary to address specific problems caused by some conditions such as "mixed" gonads that have a genuine risk of malignancy, the statement's discussion of surgery foregrounds instead cosmetic procedures aimed at "normalizing" the appearance of genitals. That the statement does not explicitly advocate cosmetic surgery is nevertheless a tremendous advance, but the significant acknowledgment that "it is generally felt that surgery that is carried out for cosmetic reasons in the first year of life relieves parental distress and improves attachment between the child and the parents" should give pause. While, as the statement admits, "the systematic evidence for this belief is lacking," cosmetic

surgery is by no means ruled out. The statement instead advises that "only surgeons with expertise in the care of children and specific training in the surgery of
DSD should undertake these procedures."[25] The fact that cosmetic genital surgery
aimed not at improving function or securing health remains so salient indicates
the extent to which medicine maintains for itself a central role in normalization, a
point that draws us back to the comparison between the histories of intersex and
homosexuality.

Normalizing Medicine

It is disappointing that the authors of the consensus statement did not assume
a more critical view of cosmetic genital surgery, but it should not be surprising.
"Normalizing" surgeries, as they are known in medicine, together with accompa-
nying hormone treatments, have constituted the standard of care for children with
intersex conditions for decades now. Originally surgical correction of genitals to
conform to sex assignment was thought to be essential to the development of a
healthy gender identity.[26] While the original rationale was famously challenged
over a decade ago, little immediate change in treatment occurred.[27] In place of
what initially appeared to be a robust theory about psychosocial development in
children was left a vague yet unrelenting concern with "normal appearance" and
the "normal life" that this appearance was supposed to promise.

   Normalization is not only a term descriptively employed by physicians for
cosmetic genital surgery in those with intersex conditions, but following the work
of Foucault, it has also become critical theoretical shorthand to signify the pervasive standards that structure and define social meaning. Norms are at once everywhere and nowhere. They are explicit and conspicuous in any number of standards
with respect to which one may be tested or assessed, with respect to body (as in
mass or function) or mind (and one's cognitive ability or deficit). They are also
unspoken, seemingly "natural," and internalized as one's "own," as is often the
case with gender norms. Whether conspicuous or not, we must reckon with the fact
that "there is," as Lennard Davis has succinctly put it, "no area of contemporary
life in which some idea of a norm, mean, or average has not been calculated."[28]

   Medicine has played a central role in the modern development of the norm,
and "medical power," as Foucault claims, "is at the heart of the society of normalization."[29] In the ancient period conceptions of health were conceived in terms
of harmonious functioning in the individual; medicine was regarded as "a set of
techniques for curing ills and of the knowledge they require."[30] This view of medicine would persist in the eighteenth century, but medicine would also come to

"embrace a knowledge of the *healthy man*, that is, a study of *non-sick man*, and a definition of the *model man*" (34; emphasis in original). Medicine assumes, in other words, a "normative posture, which authorizes it not only to distribute advice as to healthy life, but also to dictate the standards for physical and moral relations of the individual and the society in which he lives" (34).[31] The formulation of the understanding of the model man sets the stage for a further development in the nineteenth century that would see a subtle but important change from a focus on "health" to "normality." For Foucault the eighteenth-century standard of health was concerned with qualities that could be understood as specific to a particular being—namely, "vigour, suppleness, and fluidity, which were lost in illness and which it was the task of medicine to restore" (35). Such qualities were understood to a certain extent to be judged and regulated by the individual, through diet and exercise, for example, which entailed "the possibility," as Foucault writes, "of being one's own physician" (35)—the possibility, that is, that the evaluation of an individual's health could be determined and regulated only with respect to and by oneself, rather than a measure or command imposed from without. Nineteenth-century health, by contrast, "was regulated more in accordance with normality than with health; it formed its concepts and prescribed its interventions in relation to a standard of functioning and organic structure." Consequently, Foucault writes, the medicine that previously took as its object "the structure of *the organized being*" was transformed into "the *medical bipolarity of the normal and the pathological*" (35; emphasis in original). It was no longer the judgment of the individual that mattered most, but that of "experts" who would be authorized to evaluate and treat the individual as prevailing standards dictated.

Consistent with Foucault's periodization, Alice Dreger has detailed the nineteenth-century development of the taxonomic system used to classify hermaphroditic "types." This taxonomy has persisted until today, and the change in nomenclature is intended to correct its misleading and confusing emphasis on gonadal anatomy (once understood to be linked to gender identity and sexual behavior), and to reflect current understandings of the diversity of intersex conditions and their specific features.[32] According to the old taxonomy, "normal" females and males were defined as presenting only standard female or male anatomy, respectively, while so-called male and female pseudohermaphrodites and true hermaphrodites presented different kinds of mixtures of male and female anatomy.[33] Such divisions, together with the medical practices aimed to "correct" the abnormalities they denoted, may be understood to exemplify the "art of punishing," a critical component of the society of normalization:

the art of punishing . . . is aimed neither at expiation, nor even precisely at repression. It brings five distinct operations into play: it refers individual actions [or bodies, in the field of medicine] to a whole that is at once a field of comparison, a space of differentiation and the principle of a rule to be followed. It differentiates individuals from one another, in terms of following the overall rule: that the rule be made to function as a minimal threshold, as an average to be respected or as an optimum towards which one must move. It measures in quantitative terms . . . the "nature" of individuals. It introduces, through this "value-giving" measure, the constraint of a conformity to be achieved. Lastly, it traces the limit that will define difference in relation to all other differences, the external frontier of the abnormal.[34]

The language of "punishment" may seem out of place with respect to treatment of intersex conditions. It would be farfetched indeed to claim that parents or even doctors are punishing children for their difference. Yet, accounts of adults reflecting on their experiences as they grew up strongly suggest a subjection to a "punitive operation" consistent with the exercise of power Foucault so vividly describes in *Discipline and Punish*. Consider sociologist Sharon Preves's interview with Tiger, who reports having had sixteen surgeries to correct hypospadias, spending most of his summer vacations in the hospital while friends went to camp or on family vacations.[35] Others recount chilling experiences of repeated displays made of their bodies in hospitals and public clinics. Carol was humiliated by what she called the "parades" of physicians, residents, and interns — in one visit she counted more than one hundred — who "touched, poked, looked, mumbled, and left" (67). Anthropologist Katrina Karkazis's interviews with adults recount the stern proscriptions they received against questions or comments about their surgically corrected bodies; others who had surgery as young adults report the performance of surgeries without their consent, making one twelve-year-old feel, in her word, "freakish."[36]

Rather than an action undertaken intentionally (whether willingly or reluctantly) by physicians and parents, however, what Foucault means by punishment here is better captured in the passive voice, referring not to an action intended by a particular agent or agents but to an action occurring *through* them. The "offense" that provokes the punishment in the first place is itself similarly construed. Rather than conceived as a wrongdoing committed by an individual, normalization acts on "the whole indefinite domain of the non-conforming" — for example, failing to achieve a certain level of performance or, as in the case of intersex, being born with atypical anatomy.[37] By contrast to the more familiar conception of a "judicial penalty" (183), this "penalty of the norm" is more helpfully understood as a new "rationality," a way to make sense of practices and bodies that insists on homogeneity and so both fixates on—and aims to correct—individual differences figured as abnormal (199). The operation of normalization here exemplifies Foucault's provocative characterization of power as "both intentional and nonsubjective": "There is no power," he claims, "that is exercised without a series of aims and objectives. But this does not mean that it results from the choice or decision of an individual subject."[38]

This operation of power that establishes, as Foucault writes, "the Normal . . . as a principle of coercion" is evident in the standards of phallic size first discussed outside medicine by Suzanne Kessler and mordantly represented in the "phall-o-meter" distributed by the Intersex Society of North America early in its formation.[39] According to the standard then current through the 1990s, a clitoris larger than one centimeter would require cosmetic reduction, while a baby with a penis smaller than one inch at birth would be reassigned female. Between the areas of less than one centimeter and greater than one inch lay precisely this domain of nonconformity that was so disturbing as to prompt the treatment that would otherwise be regarded as a gross violation of children, physical and emotional. One might ask to whom these bodies were disturbing. From parents' accounts, it is not at all clear that they themselves were disturbed; rather, reports suggest that they were worried about how *other people* would regard their children. In other cases it appears that it was doctors who instructed parents that their children had a problem that merited correction and made threats posed as questions about how others—members of the family or caregivers who would change diapers or, in the case of boys, the peers who would be so ruthless in the locker room—would see their child.[40]

When criticisms of cosmetic genital surgeries too narrowly cast their concerns in terms of the repressive power of normalization, they ignore a critical dimension of this power as Foucault describes it.[41] In *Discipline and Punish*, he insists that "we must cease once and for all to describe the effects of power in negative terms: it 'excludes,' it 'represses,' it 'censors,' it 'abstracts,' it 'masks,' it 'conceals.' In fact, power produces; it produces reality; it produces domains of objects and rituals of truth. The individual and the knowledge that may be gained of him belong to this production."[42] Even as we must be vigilant in efforts to resist the effects of a normalizing power that has led to the classificatory systems that have wrought so much harm, we must acknowledge the fact that these very efforts are also constitutive of power. Foucault elaborates on this point in the first volume of the *History of Sexuality*, finding in the production of homosexuality an exemplary case:

> There is no question that the appearance in nineteenth century psychiatry, jurisprudence, and literature of a whole series of discourses on the species and subspecies of homosexuality, inversion, pederasty, and "psychic hermaphroditism" made possible a strong advance of social controls . . . but it also made possible the formation of a "reverse" discourse: homosexuality began to speak in its own behalf, to demand that its legitimacy or "naturality" be acknowledged, *often in the same vocabulary, using the same categories by which it was medically disqualified*.[43]

If the "normalization" of the homosexual by nineteenth-century medicine marked the production of a new limit of abnormality, and with it the abnormal individual, twentieth-century resistance to this process must likewise be understood in these terms but in reverse—as an effort, that is, to recast normalcy, to understand *as normal* this new person the homosexual, and eventually those who would identify as LGBT. The recasting of normalcy in this case would, as Foucault suggests, make use of the medical category, not in the sense of the one constricting norm against which all should be evaluated, but to understand homosexual orientation in the "older" sense of the individual standard of health that nevertheless remains active in, and provides significant validation of, current conceptions of normality. In short, the normalizing power that produced this individual as an object of the burgeoning business of psychiatric medicine produced—"improbably," "spontaneously," in Foucault's words (96)—Gay Pride and Rainbow Families, the Human Rights Campaign, and GenderPAC.

In turning once more to the history of homosexuality we should take care not to overlook the fuller picture that the history of normalization portrays, together with the lessons it teaches. Among these is the lesson that normalization "makes up people," as Hacking, following Foucault, puts it. "Making up people," Hacking writes, "changes the space of possibilities for personhood."[44] In the case of LGBT people, it seems, Hacking's point is obviously borne out, but not in any straightforward way. Where the pathological production of "the homosexual" once only limited the possibilities for personhood, it has since proven both to expand and to limit in new ways those possibilities.[45] Gay and lesbian adults have found in the United States comparatively greater "freedoms" in becoming subjects of law, politics, and ordinary social discourse. Almost daily reports on the status to pass legislation banning discrimination in employment, the adoption of children, or the right to marry are testament to how the pathologizing label "homosexual" produced the possibility for those so marked to throw off the imputation of psychiatric disease and to demand social and political recognition. Nevertheless if adults may find in the claiming—or "reclaiming"—of gay identity what we might understand as enhanced possibilities for action, we will not find at this point a similarly expanded space of possibilities for children. The suspicion that a child has "homosexual tendencies," for example, may result in treatment for gender identity disorder. In teenagers it can result in psychiatric institutionalization or in being cast out from one's family. In examining criticisms of the DSD nomenclature as pathologizing, then, we must carefully attend to the normalizing assertion that a person with an intersex condition is, or should historically be understood as, a "kind" of person.

Histories of hermaphroditism suggest that people with unusual sexual anatomies have been treated as kinds of persons, and as Chase has written, "the older terms 'intersex' and 'hermaphrodite' clearly label the person, not a medical condition that the person has."[46] Many of those critical of the new nomenclature appear to accept without reflection that persons with intersex conditions are a "type" of person, and so regard as normalizing the "pathologization" putatively entailed by the new nomenclature, yet not the very historical production of the "hermaphrodite." That is, critics seem to take for granted that there is this person, the hermaphrodite, a natural kind, but regard medicalization as a political instrument of repression. For Foucault at least there is no ground to maintain that medicalization of intersex is normalizing but that the assertion of an intersex "identity" is not. If normalization shapes what he terms the "grid of intelligibility of the social order," we must understand *both* the medicalization of intersex, as well as the production of the figure of the hermaphrodite, whether in history or today's intersex activist (the "hermaphrodite with attitude"), to be counted among normalization's effects.[47] Criticisms of the new nomenclature, and particularly those that suggest the language of "variation" or even "divergence," seem to suggest that there is some space outside or beyond normalization, but if it truly constitutes the grid of intelligibility, then we will find no such space.[48] We must come to terms instead with our reliance on this grid—on the way that conceptions of the normal and the abnormal shape the way we see and understand, what and how we know, and so paradoxically how we may resist practices by what might be understood as a literal reformation of these conceptions.

The implicit claim of LGBT activists is that a healthy sexuality or gender identity cannot be defined in the narrow nineteenth-century terms that divided normal from abnormal, heterosexual from homosexual, but must be understood in terms of the individual and what is right—that is, what is normal—for her. What this provisional victory suggests is that even as the effects of normalization can be resisted, that very resistance occurs within the terms it defines and by which it is defined in turn. We should not mistake the "depathologization" of homosexuality (its removal from the *DSM*) and the increasing acceptance of LGBT individuals as a triumph against this power, which is "everywhere," but acknowledge it as a moment that vividly illustrates that "where there is power, there is resistance, and yet, or rather consequently, this resistance is never in a position of exteriority in relation to power."[49] In looking to the history of homosexuality, then, we should not forget that resistance runs in multiple directions. The depathologization of homosexuality is notoriously linked to the development of the diagnosis of gender identity disorder, widely understood as an effort to "prevent" the development of homosexuality (and later, transsexuality) in children.[50] And we know that the idea that there could be "a hermaphrodite" whose sexual identity could confound the clear boundaries separating man and woman, boy and girl, gave impetus to the idea that such aberrations could be surgically corrected, and that children with unambiguous gender identities and normal sexual desires would result.

While we might understand the significant harm caused by these surgeries to have played an important role in producing the intersex activist, it is not at all clear that people with intersex conditions themselves agree that they are a type of person because they have a given condition or because they suffered a particular harm. Nor is it clear that promoting acceptance of intersex as an identity is necessarily an effective strategy for advancing the health and well-being of people with intersex conditions, adult or child. It was arguably this notion that a condition—whether manifested in ambiguous genitalia or a karyotype that does not in some way correspond to morphology—denoted a "kind" of person, which led to the understanding of intersex as what could be called a *disorder like no other*.

Physicians have long regarded intersex conditions as urgent problems of gender and genitalia, framed as the most significant components of identity since the nineteenth century.[51] Working to effect a "normal" gender identity (in some cases through cosmetic genital surgery, but in other cases, such as those concerning androgen insensitivity or cloacal exstrophy, through deception of affected individuals and sometimes even their families), doctors' collective aim seems to have been preventing the consolidation of any identity other than that of standard male or female. In focusing as they have on questions of gender and genitalia, and so by extension on questions of personal identity, physicians have treated intersex in ways that defy most conventional understandings of ethical medical practice: how else can we see the awarding of a prize by the Canadian Medical Association for the argument that the truth of a patient's (abnormal) condition—the knowledge of which must be essential to her participation in her own medical care—be withheld from her?[52] Is there another case in which one can imagine a physician claiming—on the invitation of a prestigious medical journal, no less—that cosmetic surgery to achieve a more normal appearance is necessary to secure a parent's love?[53] It is precisely medicine's treatment of intersex conditions as "disorders like no other" that permits the routine violation of established ethical principles that would be unthinkable in other areas of medical practice.[54] Such instances must certainly be regarded as egregious effects of the power of normalization. But what if instead of resisting medicalization we were to insist instead that physicians treat intersex "normally," that is, not as rare and unusual cases that justify extraordinary practices but as *disorders like many others*?

Some may balk at the language of "disorder." To the extent that "disorder" is taken to apply to a person who would consequently be considered "disordered" (as it most certainly was in the case of homosexuality), rather than a condition that one has (as is the case in any number of disorders for which the term gives no pause), then there is good reason to take issue with the term or, more precisely, to challenge its employment in certain contexts. Sexual orientation does not need "fixing"; gender identity and genital appearance similarly require no intervention. What—ironically perhaps—makes intersex a condition like no other is that it has been treated both by physicians aiming to "correct" the condition and by many of the activists who have resisted these same practices as an issue of identity—as the "problem" of gender and genitalia that has marked its medicalization since the nineteenth century. At the same time, intersex conditions occupy an almost entirely uncontroversial—but for that no less normalizing—medical terrain that has been inconsistently addressed by physicians and activists alike. These include hormone changes related to a given condition that may threaten an individual's well-being; more starkly, intersex conditions can and indeed have distracted physicians from detecting serious illnesses that might have been obvious in other cases. Granting that the medical cannot be neatly disentangled from the social, stakeholders in the debate over nomenclature can nevertheless agree that there are distinctions between the cultural issues of identity in which medicine has intervened and narrower matters of health, be they urgent in the case of a newborn with salt-losing CAH, or longer term, as is the case with different kinds of hormone replacement or special vulnerabilities to other conditions over the lifespan. Proponents for "demedicalization" of intersex conditions have focused principally on social issues and have not considered seriously the fact that attention to the important needs of affected individuals to receive health care attentive to their conditions is something that requires the application of a "pathologizing" term, be it disease, disorder, or injury—the only categories that authorize medical intervention.[55]

If the change in nomenclature can promote the important development of attention to the genuine health issues associated with many intersex conditions, and so displace the concerns with sexual identity, then intersex can be counted among the many disorders for which the terms *normal* and *abnormal* are taken to mark differences—some consequential and others less so—in the functioning of human bodies. We do not question the characterization of cancer as an abnormal division of cells, for example; those with thyroid disorders like Hashimoto's are grateful for the normalization of thyroid hormone levels treatment can bring. The operation of normalization in producing the distinctions between the normal and the abnormal in these cases forcefully illustrates how this power must be recognized not only to promote docility but to enhance a subject's capacities as well.

In *Self-Transformations*, Cressida Heyes helpfully draws critical theoretical attention to those "positive" aspects of normalizing power toward which Foucault gestures in *Discipline and Punish* and the first volume of *The History of Sexuality*, but does not emphasize until his subsequent work focusing on "care of the self."[56] While the power Foucault earlier described aims to limit possibilities for action, to train or "discipline" bodies to perform in certain ways and to produce particular effects, this power works at the same time to enhance capabilities in those same bodies; as Foucault writes, "the body that is manipulated, shaped, trained, which obeys [and] responds, becomes skilful and increases its forces."[57] Foucault's example of the young student assigned the repetitive writing of lines or the military man doing his drills are the classic examples; his analysis applies just as well, however, to the person managing diabetes, who must work to maintain normal levels of insulin through a whole variety of disciplinary means: controlling her diet, maintaining an appropriate level of exercise, taking and testing her blood, and of course submitting herself to specialists who will evaluate the results, prescribe additional measures or medications, and thus refine the treatment regimen. Success in managing her disorder can prevent any number of complications of diabetes, including heart attack or stroke, blindness or limb amputation, and will surely result in "the increase in capabilities [*capacités*] often interpreted by a liberal political tradition simply as the increase in autonomy."[58] The goal of effective management of diabetes is, in short, the living of a "normal" life—that is, a life as free as possible from the serious risks of the condition that would generally be taken to hamper human flourishing.[59]

What the change in nomenclature can promise, though obviously not guarantee, is the possibility that DSDs could be similarly regarded. To the extent that the effects of a given DSD curtail one's capacities and so impede one's projects, it should be understood as a disorder like any other, and appropriate treatment offered. But if the effects of a DSD are benign or might be understood to provoke concerns that would be understood as social rather than medical, then psychosocial support should be offered. This is the intervention most urgently needed for parents of newly diagnosed newborns or children who may require assistance in grappling with diagnoses of DSDs, both because, as we know from the experience of parents of children diagnosed with any number and variety of congenital disorders, parents frequently need support when, in Dreger's words, they "have the child they weren't expecting" and also because, as we know from adults with DSDs, it is not the medical condition or even the social stigma associated with having atypical anatomy that causes psychic pain, but the projection of the stigma onto them by their parents and physicians.[60] We should, in other words, seek to recast what it means to "normalize intersex conditions": we need no longer understand normalization to entail the surgical correction of so-called ambiguous genitalia but the treatment of intersex conditions as disorders like any other.

Conclusion

The comparison between intersex and homosexuality has a long history. If I have suggested here that this history is a fraught one, it is because it has functioned at so many levels both to extend and to limit understanding of the treatment of intersex conditions and the effects of that treatment for affected individuals. Medical treatment of intersex conditions for the better part of the last century has indubitably constituted another chapter in the story of modern medicine's role in the pathological production of individuals, a chapter that has followed directly on that of the making of the homosexual. At the same time, too-close identification of homosexuality with intersex has led intersex activists and their allies to ignore the underlying health conditions that may result in atypical anatomies. Employment of the DSD nomenclature, I have argued, can "normalize" in a positive sense intersex conditions by directing attention to appropriate and ethical treatment, and away from the issues of identity that are not—as the history of the treatment of homosexuality has taught us so well—the business of medicine. All this is to say that in evaluating the proper treatment of intersex conditions we must look not only to the history of homosexuality with which it has been problematically identified but to the history and contemporary treatment of other conditions as well. In the history of tuberculosis we find that social prejudice can shape medical practice in harmful ways; in diabetes and other endocrinological or metabolic disorders we may find conditions that have a good deal more in common physiologically with intersex than homosexuality and can provide models of care. Foucault's analysis of normalization, I believe, can help us distinguish between the "crushing effects of normalization" entailed by treatment and those effects of normalization that enable human beings by providing enhanced capacities.[61] In clarifying that the underlying conditions of DSDs must be the object of treatment, I have argued, the new nomenclature can be normalizing in this latter sense. If in so doing it works to produce disciplinary effects on the physicians providing treatment in the care of infants, children, and the adults they grow up to be, then medicine will once more assume its traditional role in promoting human flourishing.

Notes

I am grateful to many who have read and commented on earlier versions of this essay, including Debra Bergoffen, Carolyn Betensky, Deborah Cohen, Eileen Findlay, Katrina Karkazis, Bo Laurent, Karmen MacKendrick, Edgardo Menvielle, Iain Morland, Andrea Tschemplik, Gail Weiss, and two anonymous reviewers. I owe special thanks to Iain Morland for his sustained interest and generous readings, and to the American Association of University Women for its generous support.

1. Despite its prevalence it is important to note that *intersex* was never formally adopted by physicians as a diagnostic term. On the change in nomenclature, see I. A. Hughes et al., "Consensus Statement on Management of Intersex Disorders," *Archives of Disease in Childhood* 91 (2006): 554–63. For a discussion of the history of the development of the nomenclature, see Ellen K. Feder and Katrina A. Karkazis, "What's in a Name? The Controversy over 'Disorders of Sex Development,'" *Hastings Center Report* 38, no. 5 (2008): 33–36.

2. See, for example, Marie-Noëlle Baecheler, letter to the editor, *Archives of Disease in Childhood* (2006), adc.bmj.com/cgi/eletters/91/7/554#2562; David Cameron, letter to the editor, *Archives of Disease in Childhood* (2006), c.bmj.com/cgi/eletters/91/7/554#2479; and Milton Diamond and Hazel G. Beh, letter to the editor, *Archives of Disease in Childhood* (2006), adc.bmj.com/cgi/eletters/91/7/554#2460. See also the documents at the site of Organisation Intersex International, www.intersexualite.org/Disorders_of_Sex_Development.html (accessed July 29, 2008).

3. Corrective genital surgeries are not entirely unique in this respect. Appearance-altering surgeries intended to enhance psychosocial health rather than physical function include limb-lengthening surgeries for children with achondroplasia, as well as secondary surgeries to improve appearance in children with cleft lip and palate. For

discussion of the ethical problems these surgeries provoke, see Erik Parens, ed., *Surgically Shaping Children: Technology, Ethics, and the Pursuit of Normality* (Baltimore: Johns Hopkins University Press, 2006).

4. Diamond and Beh, letter to the editor.

5. For example, the term *intersexual* is used by Anne Fausto-Sterling, *Sexing the Body: Gender Politics and the Construction of Sexuality* (New York: Basic, 2000), 31; and Sharon E. Preves, *Intersex and Identity: The Contested Self* (New Brunswick: Rutgers University Press, 2003), 97.

6. This is a particular problem for the majority of individuals with intersex conditions assigned female, who may be reluctant to seek gynecological care and who may be especially vulnerable to illnesses typical of aging women, including osteoporosis. See, for example, Katrina A. Karkazis, *Fixing Sex: Intersex, Medical Authority, and Lived Experience* (Durham, NC: Duke University Press, 2008), 228.

7. Jennifer Terry, "Anxious Slippages between 'Us' and 'Them': A Brief History of the Scientific Search for Homosexual Bodies," in *Deviant Bodies: Critical Perspectives on Difference in Science and Popular Culture*, ed. Jennifer Terry and Jacqueline Urla (Bloomington: Indiana University Press, 1995), 135. See also Michel Foucault, *An Introduction*, vol. 1 of *The History of Sexuality*, trans. Robert Hurley (New York: Vintage, 1990), 43, 101.

8. Michel Foucault, *Abnormal: Lectures at the Collège de France, 1974–1975*, ed. Valerio Marchetti and Antonella Salomoni, trans. Graham Burchell (New York: Picador, 2003), 67–68.

9. Terry, "Anxious Slippages," 135.

10. Fausto-Sterling, *Sexing the Body*, 72. See also Monica J. Casper and Courtney Muse, "Genital Fixations," *American Sexuality Magazine*, March 16, 2006, www.nsrc.sfsu.edu/MagArticle.cfm?Article=595&PageID=0; and Alice Domurat Dreger, *Hermaphrodites and the Medical Invention of Sex* (Cambridge, MA: Harvard University Press, 1998), 8–9.

11. In a 2004 survey of pediatric endocrinologists and urologists, a startling proportion (42 percent and 57 percent, respectively) reported that projected sexual orientation of infants informs decisions on gender assignment (D. E. Sandburg et al., "Intersexuality: A Survey of Clinical Practice," *Pediatric Research* 55, no. 4 (2004): abstract 869; cited in Karkazis, *Fixing Sex*, 142); on parental expectations, see Suzanne J. Kessler, *Lessons from the Intersexed* (New Brunswick, NJ: Rutgers University Press, 1998), 26; and Peter Hegarty and Cheryl Chase, "Intersex Activism, Feminism, and Psychology: Opening a Dialogue on Theory, Research, and Practice," *Feminism and Psychology* 10 (2000): 125–26.

12. Ronald Bayer, *Homosexuality and American Psychiatry: The Politics of Diagnosis* (Princeton: Princeton University Press, 1987).

13. Cheryl Chase, letter to the editor, *Sciences*, July–August 1993, 3; Preves, *Intersex and Identity*, 88. As Karkazis attests, gay activism and queer theory have been by no

means the only influences here; feminist as well as health care and disability activism were also important (*Fixing Sex*, 246), but I would suggest a certain priority in the influence of the gay rights movement for the reasons that I have detailed here.

14. *Hermaphrodites Speak!* dir. Cheryl Chase, Intersex Society of North America, 1996. Morgan Holmes's injunction to "seize the name 'intersexual' as our own and take away its pathologizing power" is the most direct statement of this point ("Queer Cut Bodies," in *Queer Frontiers: Millennial Geographies, Genders, and Generations*, ed. Joseph A. Boone et al. [Madison: University of Wisconsin Press, 2000], 106). Other moving and provocative examples of this sort of "coming out" and reclamation of "intersex" can be seen in the first-person narratives in the collection *Intersex in the Age of Ethics*, ed. Alice Domurat Dreger (Hagerstown, MD: University Publishing Group, 1999).

15. This change is "radical" in the sense that it challenges standard practice in nearly every respect, but we must always recall that this change asks only that physicians act in accordance with established principles of evidence-based medicine, as well as in conformity with the bioethical standards supposed to guide that practice.

16. "Gender policing" includes the treatment of young children for gender identity disorder and teenagers who have been subjected to institutionalization. For an extended discussion, see Ellen K. Feder, *Family Bonds: Genealogies of Race and Gender* (New York: Oxford University Press, 2007), 45–60.

17. In this respect, the treatment of those with intersex conditions may be compared with the medical treatment of women through much of the twentieth century, whose difference from men was disregarded in most health research, with the result that medical care provided to women was often inappropriate. For an extended discussion, see Sue V. Rosser, *Women's Health — Missing from U.S. Medicine* (Bloomington: Indiana University Press, 1994).

18. There is certainly a broad range of individuals diagnosed with intersex conditions who might seek hormone replacement. For some, hormone therapy might not be understood precisely as a "choice," given the serious risks of osteoporosis for those without gonads; others might elect hormone replacement because the function of their gonads is at odds with their gender of assignment. In the latter case there is significant overlap with those who are transgendered. For a discussion of the issues involved in medicalizing these conditions, see Judith Butler, "Undiagnosing Gender," in *Undoing Gender* (New York: Routledge, 2004), 75–101.

19. Jonathan Ned Katz, *The Invention of Heterosexuality* (New York: Dutton, 1995); Ian Hacking, "Making Up People," in *Reconstructing Individualism: Autonomy, Individuality, and the Self in Western Thought*, ed. Thomas C. Heller et al. (Stanford: Stanford University Press, 1986), 222–36. It is not the case, obviously, that homosexual practices were unrecognized before this time; Katz's claim is instead that the category of "the homosexual" (together with "the heterosexual") transformed the meaning of sexual desire and divided people along the axis normal/abnormal that the homo-/heterosexual terms consolidated and naturalized.

20. For a provocative argument on the narrative figuration of intersex, see Iain Morland, "Narrating Intersex: On the Ethical Critique of the Medical Management of Intersexuality, 1985–2005" (PhD diss., University of London, 2005).

21. Arlene B. Baratz, letter to the editor, *Archives of Disease in Childhood* (2006), adc .bmj.com/cgi/eletters/91/7/554#2590; Alice Domurat Dreger et al., "Changing the Nomenclature/Taxonomy for Intersex: A Scientific and Clinical Rationale," *Journal of Pediatric Endocrinology and Metabolism* 18 (2005): 732; and Karkazis, *Fixing Sex*, 261.

22. Hacking, "Making Up People," 227.

23. Sheila Rothman, *Living in the Shadows of Death: Tuberculosis and the Social Experience of Illness in American History* (Baltimore: Johns Hopkins University Press, 1994), 181. David Barnes's history of tuberculosis in France is also illustrative here. From the early nineteenth century, he recounts, "consumption or *phthisis* was [understood as] an individual, inscrutable, and all but random killer, probably hereditary and somehow related to passion. In the 1830s, under the July Monarchy, the disease was for the first time seen as socially discriminating, choosing its victims from certain professions and from poor neighborhoods. Beginning in the 1840s, being a consumptive woman signified in certain circles heightened sensibility and emotion as well as the redemptive power of suffering. From the late 1860s through the early 1880s, as the Third Republic established itself, the disease was possibly contagious. Around 1900, tuberculosis was a national scourge, highly contagious, lurking around every corner and symptomatic of moral decay" (*The Making of a Social Disease: Tuberculosis in Nineteenth-Century France* [Berkeley: University of California Press, 1995], 13). In the United States in the early twentieth century the spread of tuberculosis was associated with vagrancy, poverty, and immigration (Rothman, *Living in the Shadows of Death*, 191). Of the last, Alan Kraut recounts that Eastern European Jewish immigrants at midcentury were despised by racists as "tuberculous" both for their supposed susceptibility to tuberculosis and for their ability to withstand the disease (*Silent Travelers: Germs, Genes, and the Immigrant Menace* [Baltimore: Johns Hopkins University Press, 1994], 155–56).

24. Even as the preservation of privacy is taken to be paramount in medical management of intersex, we should not forget the many stories of those who have been, and continue to be, subjected to photographic sessions for purposes of research, as well as repeated exams by medical residents for educational purposes. It appears that the privacy of the family, rather than the individual patient, is at issue. It may also be that the public is being protected, of course, from the "revelation" that sex is not simply binary, but this is far from an explicit rationale for secrecy. See, for example, Kessler, *Lessons from the Intersexed*, 32.

25. Hughes et al., "Consensus Statement," 557.

26. As is now well known, this theory was advanced by John Money and his associates,

among them Joan and John Hampson, and later Anke Ehrhardt. See, for example, Joan G. Hampson, John Money, and John L. Hampson, "Hermaphrodism [*sic*]: Recommendations concerning Case Management," *Journal of Clinical Endocrinology and Metabolism* 16 (1956): 547–56; and John Money and Anke A. Ehrhardt, *Man and Woman, Boy and Girl: The Differentiation and Dimorphism of Gender Identity from Conception to Maturity* (Baltimore: Johns Hopkins University Press, 1972).

27. See Milton Diamond and H. Keith Sigmundson, "Sex Reassignment at Birth: Long-Term Review and Clinical Implications," *Archives of Pediatric and Adolescent Medicine* 151 (1997): 298–304, which revealed what would come to be known in John Colapinto's words as "The True Story of John/Joan" (*Rolling Stone*, December 11, 1997, 54–73, 92–97). See also research by William Reiner, such as "Gender Identity and Sex-of-Rearing in Children with Disorders of Sexual Differentiation," *Journal of Pediatric Endocrinology and Metabolism* 18 (2005): 549–53. Consonant with Reiner's research the consensus statement does urge greater caution in matters of sex reassignment, which has typically entailed sex reassignment of 46XY boys born with micropenis or severe hypospadias.

28. Lennard J. Davis, *Enforcing Normalcy: Disability, Deafness, and the Body* (New York: Verso, 1995), 23.

29. Michel Foucault, "The Social Extension of the Norm," in *Foucault Live: Collected Interviews, 1961–1984*, ed. Silvère Lotringer, trans. Lysa Hochroth and John Johnston, 2nd ed. (New York: Semiotext(e), 1996), 197.

30. Michel Foucault, *The Birth of the Clinic: An Archaeology of Medical Perception*, trans. A. M. Sheridan Smith (New York: Vintage, 1994), 34. See also Jacques Jouanna, *Hippocrates*, trans. Malcolm B. DeBevoise (Baltimore: Johns Hopkins University Press, 1998), 326, 331; and G. E. R. Lloyd, ed., *Hippocratic Writings*, trans. J. Chadwick (New York: Penguin, 1983), 262.

31. Davis makes more explicit than Foucault here the implication of eugenic medicine, drawing a direct line between its notorious history and the birth of the norm (*Enforcing Normalcy*, 24–38).

32. Dreger et al., "Changing the Nomenclature," 730, 732–33.

33. Dreger, *Hermaphrodites*, 35–40.

34. Michel Foucault, *Discipline and Punish: The Birth of the Prison*, trans. Alan Sheridan (New York: Vintage, 1979), 182–83.

35. Preves, *Intersex and Identity*, 31.

36. Karkazis, *Fixing Sex*, 221.

37. Foucault, *Discipline and Punish*, 179.

38. Foucault, *Introduction*, 95.

39. Foucault, *Discipline and Punish*, 184; Kessler, *Lessons from the Intersexed*, 40–44.

40. See, for example, Melissa Hendricks, "Is It a Boy or a Girl?" *Johns Hopkins Magazine*, November 1993, 12. The refrain "what about the locker room?" unfortunately

retains currency. Dreger's response to such queries is apt here: "Yes, what about the locker room? If so many people feel trepidation around it, why don't we fix the locker room? There are ways to signal to children that they are not the problems and, [surgical] normalization technologies are not the way" ("When Medicine Goes Too Far in the Pursuit of Normality," *New York Times*, July 28, 1998).

41. One such critique is Elizabeth Reis's "Divergence or Disorder? The Politics of Naming Intersex," *Perspectives in Biology and Medicine* 50 (2007): 535–43.

42. Foucault, *Discipline and Punish*, 194.

43. Foucault, *Introduction*, 101; emphasis added.

44. Hacking, "Making Up People," 229.

45. A nuanced account of this point may be found in Ladelle McWhorter's Foucauldian account of her experience in *Bodies and Pleasures: Foucault and the Politics of Sexual Normalization* (Bloomington: Indiana University Press, 1999).

46. Cheryl Chase, letter to the editor, *Archives of Disease in Childhood* (2006), adc.bmj .com/cgi/eletters/91/7/554#2546.

47. Foucault, *Introduction*, 93.

48. See, for example, Diamond and Beh, letter to the editor; and Reis, "Divergence or Disorder?"

49. Foucault, *Introduction*, 93, 95.

50. See, for example, Edgardo J. Menvielle, letter to the editor, *Journal of the American Academy of Child and Adolescent Psychiatry* 37 (1998): 243–44; and Shannon Minter, "Diagnosis and Treatment of Gender Identity Disorder in Children," in *Sissies and Tomboys*, ed. Matthew Rottnek (New York: New York University Press, 1999), 9–13.

51. Foucault, *Introduction*, 155–56.

52. Anita Natarajan, "Medical Ethics and Truth-Telling in the Case of Androgen Insensitivity Syndrome," *Canadian Medical Association Journal* 154 (1996): 568–70.

53. See the invited response to Joel Frader et al., "Health Care Professionals and Intersex Conditions," *Archives of Pediatric and Adolescent Medicine* 158 (2004): 426–28, by Erica Eugster, "Reality vs Recommendations in the Care of Infants with Intersex Conditions," *Archives of Pediatric and Adolescent Medicine* 158 (2004): 428–29.

54. The remarkable lack of evidence supporting successful outcomes of cosmetic genital surgeries and sex reassignment means that intersex surgeries are experimental procedures; in this respect these treatments take their place in a notorious history of medical experiments in the United States, including the sterilization of children diagnosed with mental illness (reviewed by the U.S. Supreme Court in *Buck v. Bell*, 274 US 200 [1927]) and the Tuskegee syphilis study from 1932 to 1972 (James H. Jones, *Bad Blood: The Tuskegee Syphilis Experiment*, rev. ed. [New York: Free Press, 1993]).

55. Medicine has certainly not been consistent in its use of nomenclature. Patricia A. Ross notes that any physical problem was long cast as "disease," and "disorder" was

introduced to distinguish physical from psychiatric conditions ("Sorting Out the Concept *Disorder*," *Theoretical Medicine and Bioethics* 26 [2005]: 136n2). Disorder has been employed far more widely than Ross suggests, however. A recent edition of a textbook for medical students and pediatricians uses the term to describe all manner of conditions that warrant medical care. Chapter headings include "Allergic Disorders," "Musculoskeletal Disorders," "Disorders of the Nervous System," and so on (Lucy M. Osborn et al., *Pediatrics* [Philadelphia: Elsevier Mosby, 2004]).

56. Cressida J. Heyes, *Self-Transformations: Foucault, Ethics, and Normalized Bodies* (New York: Oxford University Press, 2007), 64.

57. Foucault, *Discipline and Punish*, 136; see also 138.

58. Heyes, *Self-Transformations*, 77.

59. The concept of "human flourishing" is most closely associated in Western philosophy with Aristotle's treatment of *eudaimonia*, frequently translated as "happiness." I have found the concept helpful in this context precisely because the philosophical provenance of the term connotes for contemporary thinkers a concept of flourishing that is historically specific, emerging from a particular cultural context.

60. Alice Domurat Dreger, "What to Expect When You Have the Child You Weren't Expecting," in *Surgically Shaping Children: Technology, Ethics, and the Pursuit of Normality*, ed. Erik Parens (Baltimore: Johns Hopkins University Press, 2006), 253–66.

61. Heyes, *Self-Transformations*, 7.

INTERSEX PRACTICE, THEORY, AND ACTIVISM

A Roundtable Discussion

Sarah M. Creighton, Julie A. Greenberg, Katrina Roen,
and Del LaGrace Volcano

$\mathcal{T}$he growing body of work on intersex now easily spans the social sciences, humanities, various clinical specialisms, and contributions from activists and artists. Much of this work, however, lies within the boundaries of separate disciplines. This roundtable discussion seeks to bring together ideas from legal, medical, social science, artistic, and activist perspectives, as a dialogue between the four authors.

Sarah Creighton is a gynecologist who works at the Middlesex Clinic in London with a team of clinicians who treat women with atypical genital development or intersex conditions. Her published work includes studies that assess the outcomes of genital surgery as well as work that explicitly seeks to promote dialogue between clinicians and intersex adults.[1]

Julie Greenberg is a professor of law, based at the Thomas Jefferson School of Law in San Diego. Her work on gender and sexual identity has been influential worldwide.[2] Her current project, *Sex Matters: Intersexuality and the Law*, will be published in 2010 by New York University Press.[3]

Del LaGrace Volcano is a visual artist whose work engages with gender variance and whose experiences of discussing the medical treatment of intersex people have brought him/her into contact with Sarah and her colleagues in the past. Some of Del's work can be seen via his/her books and Web site.[4]

The discussion's facilitator is Katrina Roen, who approaches her research on both transgender and intersex from a social science perspective, informed by queer and feminist theorizing.[5] Her work has most recently been based in the

GLQ 15:2
DOI 10.1215/10642684-2008-136
© 2009 by Duke University Press

Institute for Health Research at Lancaster University and in the Department of Psychology at the University of Oslo.

Prior to this roundtable, Katrina and Julie had corresponded briefly, and Sarah, Katrina, and Del had met in the context of the regular Critical Sexology seminars in London. Otherwise, the four authors' work is independent of one another, and we have come together for the present discussion.

The discussion begins with each participant introducing a personal perspective on intersex, which is then used to elaborate on key issues of concern to all parties.

Sarah Creighton: From my perspective the most difficult — and most stimulating — aspects of working with intersex people are the clinical dilemmas. These are not rare; they can occur in almost every clinic. They leave you worrying at the end of the day as to whether you have done the right thing. Surgical decisions are the most tricky, as surgery is irreversible.

Del LaGrace Volcano: I call myself a "gender variant visual artist." I am reluctant to call myself intersex (without qualification) because I also recognize that my experience is quite different from most intersex people. I was not genitally mutilated, although I lived with the stigma of being not quite female enough, and the shame when my body didn't develop along typical female lines.

In 1973 I revealed to my mother that my breasts had not developed properly. The right breast was a DD cup and the left barely fit into a training bra. I went to see the surgeon Dr. Jorgensen, and I asked that he make the large right breast the same size as the very flat left breast. At no time did he say this would not be possible, but when I woke up he told me my only option would be to have an implant in the left breast. I was devastated. I wanted so much to be flat chested! Like my mother. But Dr. Jorgensen had other ideas, and with my long red hair Debby Wood did as she should and agreed to have a foreign object sewn into her body.[6]

Being a very pragmatic sort, I allowed myself to be convinced that this was my only option if symmetry was my goal. What the good Dr. Jorgensen neglected to tell anyone is that the implants would need to be checked and changed after a maximum of fifteen years. The implant stayed inside my body, rotting away, for twenty-seven years. But the die was cast; I became a woman with largish breasts. I fit the stereotype and so continued to pluck my facial hair in secret for the next twenty years.

Julie Greenberg: My work has much less of an effect on a personal level than either Del's or Sarah's work. Writing legal articles requires me to be "objective." Del can incorporate the personal into his/her art and Sarah works with patients. I work with a computer. The time that I spend exploring ideas and feelings with intersex persons affects my personal life and shapes my writing, but not in the same way that I imagine it affects Sarah and Del.

Katrina Roen: Through your work, you have each expressed concerns about the use of genital surgery for atypically sexed infants. This practice does not have reliably good outcomes, and it is criticized as being a mechanism for maintaining normative binary gender.[7] I know that although you all express concern about this surgery, you approach it from different perspectives.

JG: I think many activists in the intersex community would assert that the medically unnecessary surgical alteration of intersex infants is the most critical issue to address. The law could respond to this issue in two ways: legislatures could be asked to enact laws banning such practices, and lawsuits could be brought against physicians.

It is very unlikely that local or national legislative bodies will enact laws controlling current medical practices. Legislatures rarely interfere in medical protocols. The only jurisdiction in the United States to examine this issue carefully is San Francisco. San Francisco issued *A Human Rights Investigation into the Medical "Normalization" of Intersex People*, which declared that the standard medical approach violates the human rights of intersex patients.[8] Although I believe that protective legislation is possible, I do not believe that the legislative path will be the most effective method of addressing this issue.

DLV: So you are suggesting that the other approach would be to bring lawsuits against clinicians?

JG: Yes. The intersex community could initiate lawsuits against doctors treating intersex infants. Thus far only one jurisdiction's highest court has considered whether current medical practices could lead to legal liability. The Constitutional Court of Colombia held that intersex people constitute a minority entitled to protection from discrimination.[9] The court recognized that subjecting an intersex child to surgery may violate the child's right to autonomy and bodily integrity. It also acknowledged, however, that parents have rights to privacy and family autonomy that must be considered. Therefore the court required legal and medical communities to establish an enhanced form of parental informed consent that must be qualified and persistent.

KR: The notion of informed consent is particularly problematic when the people concerned are parents of a very young child and the situation they are faced with is complicated, unexpected, and upsetting. What does "enhanced informed consent" mean in this context?

JG: Enhanced or qualified and persistent informed consent requires full and accurate information about alternative treatment protocols and written consent on more than one occasion, over an extended time period. The court ruled that once a child passes the age of five parents no longer have the power to consent, and any decision must wait until the child reaches the age of assent — the age at which a child is deemed capable of weighing the risks and benefits of a procedure and reaching an educated decision. In other words, after age five the child's right to autonomy takes precedence over the parents' right to make decisions on behalf of their children.

DLV: I think that changing the traditional medical protocol is crucial. Certainly for the Intersex Society of North America (ISNA) the key concern is to stop unnecessary surgeries for intersex infants. I applaud and endorse their efforts. But taking a broader perspective, I would say that the main problem for both the intersex and the intergendered is societal insistence that bodies always and without fail conform to the either/or, male/female paradigm. The solution is education and activism. In many ways my own art practice is an alibi for my activism.

SC: When thinking about the key concerns expressed by intersex people, I need to begin by considering the issues presented to me by patients. In the context of my work I see adolescent and adult patients. I am a gynecologist, so I only see patients assigned female. I work in a multidisciplinary team with Lih-Mei Liao (a clinical psychologist) and Gerry Conway (an endocrinologist). The key issues for the patients that I see in my medical practice are practical concerns about the appearance of the genitals and the ability to have sexual intercourse.

The surgical issues of course differ depending on diagnosis. Some will have ambiguous genitalia, and the focus is on appearance — usually clitoral size — and vaginal creation. Some have a normal female external appearance but a shortened or absent vagina, so the focus then is on vaginal lengthening.

KR: Because you are working with adolescent girls and women, Sarah, I understand that you are concerned not only by the proportion of unsatisfactory surgical outcomes for intersex children but also by the surgical requests of adolescents and adults.

SC: One dilemma is that I feel to some extent pressured by two clearly opposing views. On one side is the belief held by most adult support groups that genital surgery is often harmful and that genital variation and difference are valuable and acceptable. On the other side is the constant pressure by society that difference is a bad thing and that all must aspire to a "normal" appearance. Patients are often deeply influenced by the latter, which drives and informs decisions they make about surgery for themselves or for affected children.

I believe that our role as doctors is to do the best for each individual patient based on the available scientific data, our clinical experience, and of course the wishes of the patient. Our role is not to try to change the opinions of society — even though they certainly need to be changed!

My hope is that by careful clinical work and publication of thoughtful research on outcomes, opinions will change gradually. However, it can be very difficult to marry the broad perspective with care of the individual. My worry is that I will try and do both and end up not helping anyone!

DLV: I feel that the key issue facing the intersexed is actually a key issue facing humanity in general: *fear of difference* and compulsory heterosexuality as well as gender normativity. For society to function as it does, it is essential that there be clear lines of demarcation between those that have (power) and those that do not. Membership in the top tiers of society is determined by how well you are able to perform gender, sexuality, class, able-bodiedness, and race. Those who rock the boat, who either cannot or will not conform to expectations, especially of what it means to be a man or a woman, are usually *not* rewarded except under extremely limited conditions. Two examples spring immediately to mind: Greyson Perry and Eddie Izzard. Perry is a heterosexual male transvestite artist, and Izzard is a heterosexual male cross-dressing comedian. Both are permitted a wide latitude because they are *entertaining* and funny, and they prop up the status quo *and* make sure we all know they are really *men* and really *heterosexual*.

KR: It seems that the "fear of difference" and seeking a "normal appearance" are central to what drives people to seek genital surgery, whether for themselves or for their children.

SC: I think that despite the great debate and the huge amount of information now available about disorders of sex development (DSDs), the women I see in my clinic are still very traditional in their aspirations toward what they see as "normality." I also think that surgery is still regarded as a powerful tool and that patients view surgery as a solution to a whole range of problems related to — and some not related to — their condition.

The whole issue of genital surgery in DSD and non-DSD women is difficult. There has been a huge increase in genital surgery for "well women," and DSDs may need to be viewed against that background, too, especially in North America and Europe. Lih-Mei and I wrote recently on this in the *British Medical Journal*.[10]

DLV: But yet the question persists and is controversial: *who counts as intersex?* What are the criteria for qualification? According to some doctors, geneticists, and other health professionals, I qualify absolutely. However, I was *not* diagnosed at birth and unless I am willing to undergo invasive surgery (a hysterectomy) to discover if I have testicular tissue in either gonad, I won't know for sure if my "condition" is classifiable under the category of intersex. A great many people have bodily symptoms that were not detected at birth or did not manifest until puberty. It has been in the interests of the medical establishment to make sure that intersex is perceived by the general public as a highly rare condition, which requires information not available or accessible to the average person. This keeps the power dynamic balanced firmly in favor of the medical establishment.

KR: So for both adults and children there are these two connected issues: definition (who counts, who gets diagnosed, for whom is surgery seen as important), and normative pressure (under what circumstances is "normalizing" cosmetic surgery seen as desirable and even necessary). The current response to both of these issues has people undergoing surgery that damages sensation, at the very least.

SC: Yes. Even though there is good evidence (mainly from our research work), that clitoral surgery damages sexual sensation and interferes with the ability to orgasm, the vast majority of the adolescent and adult women I see with an enlarged clitoris will request clitoral reduction. They do have full counseling about the risks of surgery and input from psychologists but usually prefer to risk sensation for the sake of a more "normal-looking" genital appearance.

Also, as I mentioned, a key concern for the patients we see is sexual intercourse. We seek to address this issue nonsurgically through our vaginal dilation program. About 85 percent of the women we see without prior genital surgery will achieve a vaginal length adequate for penetration. There is no noticeable difference in the sexual partner preference — women with female partners are just as motivated to lengthen their vaginas. If dilators do not work, then vaginal reconstruction surgery is the next step. Again the majority of women then choose to go ahead with surgery despite the fact that the procedures are lengthy and have risks attached.

KR: Would each of you be able to say what goals specifically need to be fought for—and at what point we can put our feet up and stop challenging the way intersex people are treated?

DLV: While stopping unnecessary surgeries for intersex children is important and I think should be a primary goal, I feel that ISNA has that covered. My own personal priority is *education* of the masses. It is only by challenging the way in which knowledge is imparted and validated, through unpacking the centuries of dualistic gender propaganda, that progress will be made.

My strategy, which seems to be effective, is to be willing to educate through entertainment, rather than browbeat people into submitting to my worldview. By positioning myself and the people with whom I work (through photography, film, or interview) as heroic subjects worthy of emulation rather than pathologized victims as the media and medical professions seem to prefer, I create the space for education to exist and, hopefully, to thrive.

JG: As long as anecdotal information is shaping medical practices, we won't be putting up our feet for some time. I find it surprising that we don't have more studies assessing the different medical protocols. Sarah could probably speak to this issue.

SC: I imagine what you mean is a prospective study looking at those diagnosed with DSD (either at birth or throughout childhood and adolescence) and following them into adult life. I am not aware of any such study. Research funding is usually allocated in two-year grants (maximum five years). Long-term research money is almost impossible to get. In addition, in the U.K., big funding bodies have given awards only to groups researching common conditions such as cancer and heart disease. Rarer conditions are not often considered.

KR: An argument that is repeatedly used to support the practice of surgically modifying intersex children's genitalia is that it is in the child's best interests. Julie's work reminds us that article 3 of the Convention of the Rights of the Child requires that the interests of the child be a primary consideration, yet debates about cosmetic genital surgery for children do not make it easy to tease out exactly what is in the best interests of the child.[11]

How would you, Julie, approach this argument about whether offering or withholding surgery might actually be "in the best interests of the child"?

JG: Whether legal institutions will even become involved in these types of cases is questionable. The most likely case a court would consider would involve a surgery that caused sterilization. In these cases the burden on the parents would be quite high because of the protected status accorded reproductive rights. A court would be hesitant to order a surgery that could *possibly* result in enhanced psychological well-being if it would eliminate a child's ability to reproduce.

However, if the surgery does not affect reproductive capacity, the result may differ. Generally courts do not intervene in medical decisions if the parents and the treating team agree. In other words, if the physicians and parents agree that the child should undergo surgery, and the procedure does not affect a fundamental right such as reproduction, a court would be unlikely to become involved in the process. First, there is the practical problem of someone having standing to bring the suit on behalf of the child. In addition, parental decision making is a highly respected right. Courts are hesitant to intervene unless the child's fundamental rights are threatened.

If we continue to allow parents to consent to nonmedically necessary surgery for their intersex infants, I believe the approach taken in Colombia is probably the wisest model we could currently adopt. Parents must be given full information about the possible dangers associated with surgery, the existence of other paradigms, and the possibility of delaying surgeries. At the same time we must ensure that adequate psychological support is provided to the children and their parents. In addition we should require, as the Colombian court did, that parental authorization must be given on several occasions, over a reasonable time period, to ensure that the parents have enough time to understand the situation and the potential consequences of their decisions.

SC: Yes, I can see how that could work in the case of parents and infants. How do you think these ideas could be extended to support optimal practice with older children and adolescents?

JG: I believe a similar model is appropriate for children who have reached the age of assent and are contemplating surgery. Age-appropriate education must be provided by a diverse group of experts who can provide thorough information about the potential emotional, physical, and sexual functioning consequences of these decisions. As your research indicates, Sarah, the desire for "attractive" genitalia is not limited to adolescents born with an intersex condition. Cosmetic genitoplasty is a booming business, and many women opt for surgery even after being informed of the risks associated with surgery, and the lack of evidence to show that it leads to enduring psychological or functional benefits.[12] Therefore we have to recognize that the desire to "fit in" may be a driving force behind the decisions of adults as well as of adolescents, and address this issue in the educational processes.

KR: This links back to Sarah's comment that the women who come to her clinic are "still very traditional in their aspirations toward what they see as 'normality.'" What kinds of alternative aspirations and ideals do you have in mind, Sarah, in your research on the clinical outcomes for intersex women, and in your clinical approach?

SC: Although reducing the numbers of women choosing genital surgery may sound sensible, I think it is too simplistic. A more useful goal would be to enable women to be more informed about the surgical choices they make and to be more realistic about precisely what surgery can and cannot achieve.

Some surgery is regarded as necessary by both clinician and patients. This relates more specifically to vaginal surgery — for example, operating to create a vagina to allow passage for menstruation or to allow penile-vaginal intercourse. What would be beneficial would be to help patients be more realistic about surgery. Women tend to see the surgery as a "cure" for their condition. Surgery can of course create a vaginal passageway for menstruation and intercourse but will also leave scarring, vaginal dryness, and sometimes soreness or pain. Dilation may be needed to keep the vagina patent (open and unobstructed). Surgical expertise cannot create a vagina that functions as if no surgery has been necessary. I think some women perceive surgery as a hurdle that must be overcome but after that everything will be "normal." I think that this has been partly the fault of clinicians in the past who have implied or said that surgery is the key to treatment that has led to unrealistic expectations.

Clitoral surgery is rather a different matter, and I would be pleased to see a reduction in the numbers of children undergoing clitoral reduction.

KR: Given that you would be pleased to see less clitoral surgery on children and that you consider that women seeking genital surgery need to be realistic about what such surgery might achieve, where are the boundaries beyond which you personally would not be willing to operate?

SC: There are patients upon whom I will not operate. This would be in cases in which I thought the surgery was unnecessary or potentially harmful. However, this is a personal choice and will vary among surgeons. Patients in that situation may seek out second opinions and thereby find someone willing to operate.

I would operate only if I were able to discuss all of the potential drawbacks of surgery, especially the impact upon sexual sensation. There is no set age for this, as girls mature at variable stages, but it's usually midadolescence. I also would not operate if I considered that the clitoris was of a "normal" size, based on my clinical experience with women with and without DSD. I do not in any event operate on babies or small children, as I am not a pediatric surgeon.

KR: This brings us back to the point that clinicians are seen as responding to individual patients' needs or requests, rather than seeking to engage in social change movements. Conversely, many intersex adults wish to bring about social change and influence the ways in which clinicians work, and these two aspects are seen by them as intertwined.

Del's Web site approaches this in a productive way, I think. On your Web site, Del, you have stated:

> As a gender variant visual artist I access "technologies of gender" in order to amplify rather than erase the hermaphroditic traces of my body. I name myself. A gender abolitionist. A part-time gender terrorist. An intentional mutation and intersex by design (as opposed to diagnosis), in order to distinguish my journey from the thousands of intersex individuals who have had their "ambiguous" bodies mutilated and disfigured in a misguided attempt at "normalization." I believe in crossing the line as many times as it takes to build a bridge we can all walk across.[13]

I particularly like the metaphor of your work building a bridge for yourself and others to walk across. This suggests an ideal to which you are aspiring through your work — perhaps an ideal that allows anyone and everyone to access possibilities of gender fluidity? If this is the case, how would you respond to the situation that Sarah presents — that women, intersexed and otherwise, do continue to aspire to gender normativity in their bodily appearance, rather than enjoying the fluidity that has become at least slightly more accessible in recent years?

DLV: I will respond by highlighting specific sentences in my artist's statement. The first concerns the point of valuing what you call "gender fluidity." The second concerns my creative approach to activism. I write that I am "a gender abolitionist. A part-time gender terrorist." I'm not really a gender abolitionist if what that means is I want to live in a world where gender does not exist. I recognize, validate, and support those that want to live a mono-gendered lifestyle. I just wish they would grant me the same privileges. I say a part-time gender terrorist because on the occasions when I do let my gender variance shine a great many people find the experience to be terrifying. They react as though gender were the last bastion of civilization as we know it. In a world where so few things are certain, people want to believe in something. They cling to the belief system called binary gender as if they were drowning in a frozen sea.

Finally, I write that "I believe in crossing the line as many times as it takes to build a bridge we can all walk across." The work I do is motivated by a desire to be part of positive social change. By using my own body and experience I have been given a voice and access to audiences around the world. I use visual beauty to seduce people into suspending absolute belief in their worldview and allowing themselves to enter into mine.

Conclusion

While this discussion offers little visual beauty, it hopefully goes some way toward building bridges. One challenge that the authors faced was finding a way to talk across the personal and professional so that we could meaningfully engage with one another, rather than talk past each other. Another challenge for this area of work more broadly concerns building bridges between the individuals and the institutions involved. The difficulties of this resonated through our discussion: Creighton pointed out the limitations of what one surgeon can decide—she cannot stop patients going elsewhere for "normalizing" surgery; Greenberg pointed out the limitations of what legislation can offer—suggesting that legislatures rarely interfere with medical protocols; Volcano pointed out the difficulties of being able to "define" oneself—when understandings of intersex hinge on medical classifications through which atypically sexed individuals may be disempowered.

Although the prior work of the four authors clearly indicates a shared commitment to change in the situation of intersex people, the mechanisms for such changes are understood differently or appear rather elusive. In our attempt to build bridges through this discussion, it becomes clear that the mechanism for change—including the issue of who may be able to take responsibility for such change—remains oddly elusive. Even with the best intentions it is hard to see substantial changes taking place without ongoing communication and collaboration across our differences in perspective and discipline.

Notes

This roundtable took place via Internet-based exchanges from June 2007 to January 2008. We would like to thank Iain Morland for initiating this collaboration.

1.   Sarah M. Creighton, Catherine L. Minto, and Stuart J. Steele, "Objective Cosmetic and Anatomical Outcomes at Adolescence for Ambiguous Genitalia Done in Childhood," *Lancet* 358 (2001): 124–25; Sarah M. Creighton et al., "Meeting between Experts: Evaluation of the First U.K. Forum for Lay and Professional Experts in Inter-

sex," *Patient Education and Counselling* 54 (2004): 153–57; Naomi S. Crouch et al., "Sexual Function and Genital Sensitivity following Feminizing Genitoplasty for Congenital Adrenal Hyperplasia," *Journal of Urology* 179 (2008): 634–38.

2. Julie A. Greenberg, "International Legal Developments Protecting the Autonomy Rights of Sexual Minorities: Who Should Determine the Appropriate Treatment for an Intersex Infant?" in *Ethics and Intersex*, ed. Sharon Sytsma (Dordrecht: Springer, 2006), 87–102; Greenberg, "Intersex and Intrasex Debates: Building Alliances to Challenge Sex Discrimination," *Cardozo Journal of Law and Gender* 12 (2005): 99–116.

3. Julie A. Greenberg, *Sex Matters: Intersexuality and the Law* (New York: New York University Press, forthcoming).

4. See, for example, Del LaGrace Volcano, *Sublime Mutations: Photographs 1990–2000* (Tübingen: Konkursbuch Verlag Claudia Gehrke, 2000); www.dellagracevolcano.com.

5. Katrina Roen, "Intersex Embodiment: When Health Care Means Maintaining Binary Sexes," *Sexual Health* 1 (2004): 127–30; Roen, "Queerly Sexed Bodies in Clinical Contexts: Problematising Conceptual Foundations of Genital Surgery with Intersex Infants," in *Sex and the Body*, ed. Annie Potts, Nicola Gavey, and Ann Weatherall (Palmerston North, New Zealand: Dunmore, 2004), 89–106; Roen, "'But We Have to Do Something': Surgical 'Correction' of Atypical Genitalia," *Body and Society* 14 (2008): 47–66.

6. "Debby Would if She Could" is a character Del created based on the name bestowed upon him/her at birth, Debra Wood.

7. Katrina Roen, "Queer Kids: Towards Ethical Clinical Interactions with Intersex People," in *Ethics of the Body: Postconventional Challenges*, ed. Margrit Shildrick and Roxanne Mykitiuk (Cambridge, MA: MIT Press, 2005), 259–78.

8. Human Rights Commission of the City and County of San Francisco, *A Human Rights Investigation into the Medical "Normalization" of Intersex People* (San Francisco: Human Rights Commission, 2005).

9. Constitutional Court of Colombia, Sentencia SU-337/99 (1999) and Sentencia T-551/99 (1999).

10. Lih-Mei Liao and Sarah M. Creighton, "Requests for Cosmetic Genitoplasty: How Should Healthcare Providers Respond?" *British Medical Journal* 334 (2007): 1090–92.

11. Greenberg, "International Legal Developments," 93.

12. Liao and Creighton, "Requests for Cosmetic Genitoplasty."

13. Del LaGrace Volcano, "Artist Statement" (2005), www.dellagracevolcano.com/statement.html.

THE HERM PORTFOLIO

Del LaGrace Volcano

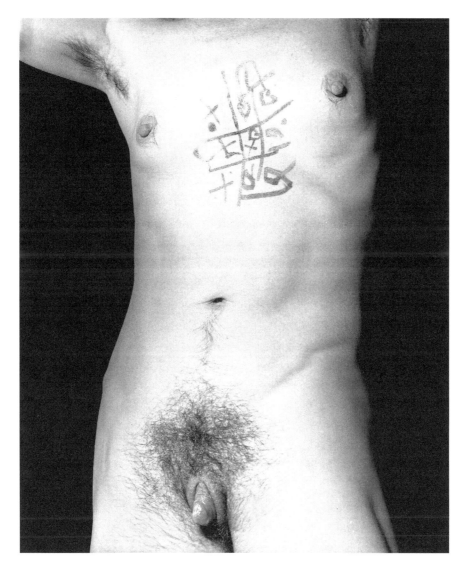

Hermaphrodite Torso, London, 1999. All images courtesy of Del LaGrace Volcano

GLQ 15:2

DOI 10.1215/10642684-2008-137

Abu Kasoum, Paris, 2005

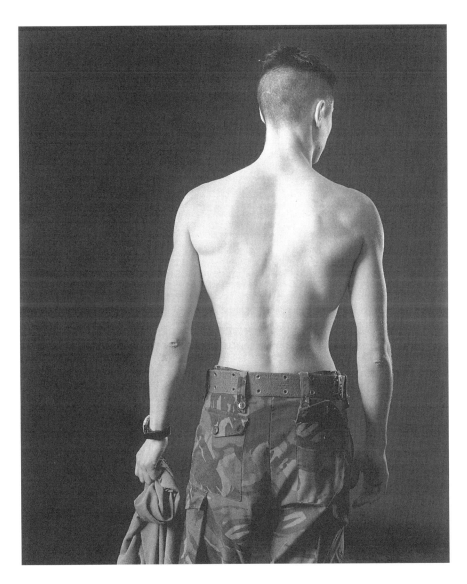

Jax Back, London, 1991

Jax Revealed, London, 1991

SubLiminal Herm, self-portrait, Barcelona, 2004

QUANTUM SEX: INTERSEX AND THE MOLECULAR DECONSTRUCTION OF SEX

Vernon A. Rosario

*J*ntersex" emerged in the 1990s, a seemingly novel phenomenon with tremendous potential in terms of cultural politics and gender theory. These congenital conditions of atypical genital and gonadal development are at the intersection of sexual biology, social gender determination, and personal identity. As such, intersex conditions challenge traditional medical and cultural principles of sex and gender. American cultural consciousness of intersex conditions arose at the nexus of several events in the 1990s: the rise of intersex activism, the rediscovery of the "John/Joan" case, and the appropriation of intersex in gender studies circles. Cheryl Chase started the Intersex Society of North America (ISNA) in 1993 as an informal support group for adults with intersex conditions.[1] ISNA grew rapidly into a highly vocal and increasingly successful lobbying group that made the American public more aware of intersex individuals and pressed the medical profession to reevaluate the treatment of patients with intersex conditions or what some have recently renamed disorders of sex development (DSDs).[2] In 2008, ISNA was dissolved, and many of those involved with it, including Cheryl Chase (under the name Bo Laurent), shifted the efforts to a new organization, the Accord Alliance, that is focused on DSD-related health care issues.

The popular media first jumped on the subject because of David Reimer, who had been discussed since the 1960s under the pseudonym John/Joan. The journalist John Colapinto described Reimer's life in a poignant biography/exposé after Reimer had been tracked down by the biologist Milton Diamond and Reimer's former psychiatrist, H. Keith Sigmundson.[3] Other journalists almost gleefully used the case to assault the psychologist John Money's theory of gender plas-

GLQ 15:2
DOI 10.1215/10642684-2008-138
© 2009 by Duke University Press

ticity and more fundamentally the concept of gender itself that Money had elaborated in the 1950s.[4] In the popular media the revised moral of the Reimer case
was that gender identity is hardwired in the brain in utero, and Money's attempts
to tinker with that neuropsychology were misguided if not frankly abusive.[5] By
extension some journalists argued that gender studies and all studies relying
on social constructionist theory were equally deluded and dangerous: "[Gender]
theory rejects the conventional notion of male and female in favor of the ambiguous concept of 'gender.' Its advocates' motto can be described as 'anatomy is not
destiny.' . . . The idea that gender is in great part socially determined led doctors
to perform the boy's second mutilation [orchiectomy]. It has in the intervening
years flowered into a reigning dogma in such academic twilight zones as Gender
Studies and its cousins."[6] Academic analysts in gender studies, on the other hand,
utilized intersexes to further the social constructionist case. Anne Fausto-Sterling
early on argued that there are not two sexes, but five.[7] Suzanne J. Kessler argued
that gender is not dichotomized but variable and that intersexes will teach us to
eliminate the category of gender altogether.[8] Judith Butler erected a straw man
argument against the biological determinants of sex by misrepresenting Diamond
as a simplistic Y chromosome determinist who supposedly argues that any infant
with a Y chromosome should be assigned or reassigned male.[9]

   Here I would like to get beyond these Manichaean debates to argue for
an analytics of gender and sexuality that takes the social and the biological seriously by acknowledging the complexity and depth of both influences. The current
molecular biology of sex determination is particularly amenable to this kind of
analysis, as is contemporary molecular genetics in general. The Mendelian one
gene – one trait model has been largely replaced by discussions of oligogenetic
and polygenetic traits: a few or many genes conferring small statistical odds for
different traits under particular environmental and developmental circumstances.
This is particularly true for complex traits.[10] However, this is not the molecular
genetics presented in the popular press. A case in point is a 2007 *New York Times*
article titled "Pas de Deux of Sexuality Is Written in the Genes."[11] In it Nicholas
Wade — by arguing against Butler — tries to explain that "human sexual behavior is not a free-form performance, biologists are finding, but is guided at every
turn by genetic programs." According to Wade this all begins in the womb at the
moment of sex determination: "In the womb, the body of a developing fetus is
female by default and becomes male if the male-determining gene known as SRY
is present. This dominant gene, the Y chromosome's proudest and almost only
possession, sidetracks the reproductive tissue from its ovarian fate and switches
it into becoming testes. Hormones from the testes, chiefly testosterone, mold the

body into male form." Despite the sexist, anthropomorphizing language of "dominance," Y-chromosomal pride, and ovarian fatalism (to which I will return), this encapsulation of sex determination presents a significant leap forward from simple chromosomal sex determination—the idea that XX chromosomes determine female sex, while XY makes a male. Wade's explanation, however, is dated and only accords with understandings of sex determination until 1990. The molecular biology of sex determination has become far more complex in the intervening years. For intersex people this molecular complexity is a matter of health as well as sex. Such biological and genetic complexity requires an ever more microscopic—actually molecular—level of understanding of sex in intersex people, and most likely for an ever-increasing number of people with undiagnosed intersex conditions or unexplained hypofertility.

Such complexity also requires a specific and comprehensive understanding, and for that I have to get into some genetic details. As I shortly demonstrate, intersex conditions are extremely diverse (see table 1), so I use the details of one person's story and intersex biology as the starting point for a broader survey of two decades of sex research. In tracing a path from the chromosomal to the molecular genetics of sex, I point out how this research has shaken off two millennia of Aristotelian sexism to arrive at an interactionist model of genetic sex modifiers that destabilize a binary model of sex in favor of a polymorphic and multifactorial model, which I call quantum sex.

Helen and *WT1*

I first met Helen for a psychiatric consultation when she was seventeen. She was an energetic girl who dressed in athletic clothes and described herself as very popular. Although she had graduated from high school, she had had a rocky academic experience because of attentional problems and defiance toward teachers. Helen and her mother concurred that Helen had always been a tomboy with an explosive temper. She also had a complex medical history, of which she had been only partly aware as a child. At age three-and-a-half her kidneys failed, and within a year she required a cadaveric kidney transplant. As a teenager she was placed on "female" hormones (Premarin and Provera), in addition to the immunosuppressant medications required to sustain her transplant.

It was only at fifteen that she learned of her underlying diagnosis. Unfortunately her mother had revealed this during a fight after discovering love letters from a girl to Helen. Maybe she liked girls, mom blurted out, because she had been born a boy! Soon after this Helen learned that she had been diagnosed in

Table 1. Estimated Frequency of Intersex-Related Diagnoses

Cause	Estimated frequency/ 100 live births
Non-XX and non-XY (except Turner and Klinefelter)	0.0639
Turner (X)	0.0369
Klinefelter (XXY)	0.0922
Subtotal for chromosomal difference	0.193
Androgen insensitivity syndrome	0.00760
Partial androgen insensitivity syndrome	0.000760
Classical congenital adrenal hyperplasia (CAH)	0.00770
Late onset CAH	1.5
Subtotal for known hormonal causes	1.516
Vaginal agenesis	0.0169
True hermaphrodites (ovotestes)	0.0012
Idiopathic	0.0009
Total (aside from hypospadias)	1.728
Hypospadias	1.87 ± 1.105

Source: Adapted from Melanie Blackless et al., "How Sexually Dimorphic Are We? Review and Synthesis," *American Journal of Human Biology* 12 (2000): 159, 160.

Note: These figures present an upper-limit estimate of the prevalence of all intersex diagnoses organized into three main classes of disorders. Hypospadias is an extremely common male birth defect; however, third-degree hypospadias with genital ambiguity is rare. Leonard Sax has pointed out that these figures overrepresent the frequency of intersex by including the full prevalence of diagnoses (such as congenital adrenal hyperplasia), which only present with genital ambiguity in severe cases. Sax's more conservative estimate of the prevalence of genital ambiguity and "sex reversal" (discordant sex chromosomes and genitalia) is 0.018 percent of live births ("How Common Is Intersex? A Response to Anne Fausto-Sterling," *Journal of Sex Research* 39 [2002]: 174–78).

infancy with Denys-Drash syndrome (DDS). She had a 46XY chromosomal karyotype, and in her first year of life had undergone a laparotomy during which dysfunctional testes were removed to prevent later testicular cancer. She was found to have a vagina but no uterus. Two years later she underwent so-called corrective reduction of her clitoris.

DDS is characterized by a 46XY karyotype with ambiguous genitalia, but in 40 percent of cases there are completely unremarkable female external genitalia.[12] Renal disease usually begins in the first year of life, and there is a high frequency of Wilms' tumor of the kidney. In 1990 Wilms' tumor was found to be associated with mutations in a gene that was named *WT1* (Wilms' tumor-1).[13] The protein product of *WT1* was found to be a group of DNA-binding proteins that act as transcriptional activators or repressors (they turn particular genes on or off) depending on cellular environment and other genetic factors.[14] Given that a mutation in *WT1* was associated with tumors, it was presumed to be a tumor-suppressor gene. Since 1991, however, genetic studies of DDS patients have found that DDS is also associated with *WT1* point mutations (of a single DNA base pair).[15] So *WT1* is a gene not only associated with testicular cancer but also essential for testicular development and male sex determination. Thirty-four different critical mutations in *WT1* have been found to be associated with female genital development in XY individuals.[16] But the curious thing is that *WT1* is not on the so-called sex chromosomes, X and Y. *WT1* is on the short arm of chromosome 11 (11p13), one of the autosomes (chromosomes other than X or Y). To understand how researchers arrived at this conundrum of sex-determining genes on non-sex-chromosomes, we need to review a century of sex determination research and its underlying sexist hypotheses.

From Bisexual Gonads to *SRY*

The biological difference between the sexes versus their transmutability has been debated since antiquity.[17] Comparative anatomists in the mid-nineteenth century had discovered that, at very early stages of mammalian embryonic development, immature gonadal and genital tissues look identical in males and females. Victorian sexologists would therefore write of the "bisexuality" of the mammalian embryo.[18] At this developmental stage, the genital and gonadal tissue is therefore described (even in current biological literature) as "indifferent." The primordial genital tissue can develop into labia majora or fuse as a scrotum, while the phallus can take on clitoral or penile appearance. Internally, primordial gonadal tissue develops into ovarian or testicular tissue (and extremely rarely a mixture of these). The embryo is also "bisexual" in terms of the genital ductal system; however, these are *parallel* systems rather than derived from the same tissue. In other words, *both* the Müllerian ducts and the Wolffian ducts are present at an early stage in development, with subsequent degeneration of one of the two ductal systems.[19] It is only by the second month postconception in humans that there usually is differentiation into typical female or male sexual anatomy.[20]

What makes most embryos develop in one direction or the other? Fin de siècle biologists widely believed that environmental factors (such as temperature and nutrition) determined sex.[21] The first suggestion of a connection between chromosomes and sex was published by H. Henking in 1891.[22] In the fire bug, *Pyrrhocortis apterus*, Henking noted that the female had twenty-four chromosomes, while the male seemed to have twenty-three. Uncertain whether this solitary structure (which he called a "nucleolus") was an additional chromosome, he labeled it *X* in his drawing (leading to the term *X chromosome*). He noted that *P. apterus* spermatozoa came in two varieties: those with and those without the "nucleolus." Following on Henking's discovery, Clarence E. McClung made the bold hypothesis that this "nucleolus" was not just an effect of sex determination but the cause of it. He proposed that the "nucleolus" is a sex-determining "accessory chromosome" carried on the "motile" spermatozoa—not the "passive" ova—and "is the bearer of those qualities which pertain to the male organism."[23]

Gregor Mendel's pioneering studies from the 1860s of trait inheritance in peas were only rediscovered in 1900. Sex determination by chromosomes—following Mendelian inheritance patterns—was demonstrated soon thereafter by Nettie Maria Stevens and Edmund Beecher Wilson. In 1905, Stevens described the small and large sex chromosomes in the mealworm, which has an XX/XY sex chromosome system (as in mammals).[24] The same year Wilson described how in the squash bug, *Anasa tristis*, the female has twenty-two chromosomes, while the male has twenty-one (a 22,X/21,0 sex chromosome system).[25] Wilson's discovery not only challenged but inverted McClung's theory that males bear the sex-determining chromosomal factor. In the squash bug it is the female that has the supplemental chromosome. After Stevens's and Wilson's work, chromosomal sex determination became increasingly widely accepted among biologists, and further studies in different species demonstrated that there are a variety of sex chromosome systems among animals.[26]

If one pair of chromosomes differs between male and female mammals, it was a logical hypothesis that these "sex chromosomes" determined sex because they contained sex-determining genes. Since mammalian males (XY) and females (XX) both have at least one X chromosome, the Y chromosome seemed to be a likely site for a male-determining gene. The French physiologist Alfred Jost discovered that by transplanting testes into rabbit embryos (whether XX or XY) he could force male sexual development.[27] Conversely, removal of gonadal tissue before its differentiation into testes would lead to female differentiation of the remaining reproductive system. Jost therefore proposed that there was a testis-determining factor (TDF) that first triggered the differentiation of the bipotential gonad into a testicle. After this, the testicle produced other hormones that would direct the further differentiation of the reproductive system in a male direction. Thus Jost conceptually divided the embryology of sex into two stages: "sex determination" (inducing testis formation) and "sex differentiation" (subsequent differentiation of the internal and external reproductive system).[28]

Jost's hypothesis follows a neo-Aristotelian philosophy of sex: males require an *active* process to develop (the TDF), whereas female development occurs *passively* and by default (because of the maternal hormonal milieu). Aristotle in *Generation of Animals* presented the two sexes as being of distinct principles: the male contains the "principle of movement and generation," while the female contains the principle of "matter."[29] The female semen (menstrual fluid) contributes the *material* of the embryo, which is given *form* by the male semen because it alone possesses the principle of soul (ψυχη). For Aristotle, the female is "as it were a mutilated male" (737a25). It is the male who contributes the active component that leads to the greater vital heat necessary for the formation of a male fetus. If the father is healthy and not too young or too old he will produce stronger, more active male semen that is more likely to prevail over the female material and thereby generate male offspring (776b30).[30] McClung's accessory chromosome model similarly had a neo-Aristotelian foundation: male sex determination needs supplemental active genetic intervention, while a female outcome is the result of a genetic deficit. Jost's developmental model was explicitly testocentric: some active supplemental genetic influence is needed to trigger testis formation, whereas the ovary is relegated to being a default organ requiring no particular genetic machinery worthy of investigation. This is still the philosophical underpinning of Wade's summary of sex determination in his 2007 *New York Times* article.

Until the 1990s, geneticists searched the Y chromosome for a testis-determining gene to the neglect of ovarian development. The science historian Sarah S. Richardson highlights how women biologists such as Eva M. Eicher, Linda L. Washburn, and Fausto-Sterling in the mid-1980s highlighted the sexism underlying the research agenda of searching for a testis-determining gene on the Y chromosome — or what I call the testocentric hypothesis.[31] After many false leads, molecular biologists in 1990 identified a testis-determining gene on the Y chromosome and named it *SRY* (sex-determining region of the Y).[32] It was identified thanks to rare intersex individuals who are XX males or XY females because *SRY* crossed over from the Y to the X chromosome during spermatogenesis.

Subsequent *Sry* transfection experiments in mice confirmed that it was a testis-determining gene, since it could induce testicle formation in XX mice. Like *WT1* in humans, the *Sry* gene in mice was found to code for a protein (labeled

SRY) that binds DNA, causing it to bend at a specific angle that may help facilitate transcription (from the DNA code to RNA and eventually a protein).[33] The gene is active in the developing mouse gonadal ridge during a short critical period in development when the indifferent gonad takes the step toward developing as a testis. It is still not understood, however, what exactly the *SRY* protein product *does* to induce testicular development.

The discovery of *SRY*—the "dominant gene" and "the Y chromosome's proudest possession," as Wade put it—did not finally solve the mystery of sex. Instead, actual intersex individuals in all their diversity confounded the elegant simplicity of the testocentric model—initiating its rapid deconstruction. With *SRY* identified and genetic testing significantly simpler and cheaper in the 1990s, subsequent genetic studies of intersexed people found that there are 46XX individuals with testes who do *not* possess the *SRY* gene, suggesting that some other gene or genes can induce testis determination in the absence of *SRY*. Geneticists also discovered 46XY individuals with ovaries who have duplication of an X chromosome gene labeled *DAX-1*, which if present in a double dose can override *SRY*-stimulated testis development. Subsequent research has suggested that *WT1* increased expression of the *SRY* gene.[34] Researchers hypothesize that *SRY* is involved in a double inhibition pathway—repressing a subsequent factor that represses maleness.[35]

Rapid advances in the genetics of sex determination have completely trashed the 1950s notion that the human Y chromosome alone determines male sex. At this point genes from chromosomes 9 (*SF-1*), 11 (*WT-1*), 17 (*SOX-9*), 19 (*MIS*), and the X chromosome (*DAX-1*) in addition to *SRY* on the Y chromosome (or sometimes on the X) are essential for the usual development of testes and male internal and external genitalia (see table 2). Further, these genes' proteins have multiple sites of action beyond the gonads. *SRY*, for example, appears to be consistently expressed in mammals around the time of testis differentiation, but in different mammal species is expressed in other tissues at other times. Its function is not limited to testis determination; therefore its name, like that of so many genes—such as Wilms' tumor-1—is a misnomer as well as a historical artifact just like the "sex chromosomes" and the "sex hormones."[36] What is more, at every step of these genes' action there are critical points where the effects of environment, particularly neighboring tissue and gene expression, modulates or thwarts their usual functions. Most dramatically, many reptiles and some fish lack sex chromosomes entirely, and sex is determined by environmental factors such as temperature.[37]

Table 2. Genes Involved in Mammalian Sex Determination

Gene	Chromosomal localization	Putative function	Phenotype of mutations
SF-1	9q33	Transcription factor	XY gonadal dysgenesis and adrenal insufficiency
WT-1	11p13	Transcription factor	Denys-Drash and Frasier syndromes
SRY	Yp11.3	Transcription factor	Feminized XY and gonadal dysgenesis
DAX1	Xp21.3	Transcription factor	Duplication: XY gonadal dysgenesis Mutation: adrenal hypoplasia congenita
SOX9	17q24	Transcription factor	Duplication: masculinized XX Mutation: campomelic dysplasia with XY gondal dysgenesis
M33	17q25	Transcription factor	Feminized XY
Fgf9	13q11–13	Signaling molecule	Feminized XY and gonadal dysgenesis
DMRT1	9p24.3	Transcription factor	Deletion: feminized XY, gonadal dysgenesis, microcephaly, mental retardation
AMH	19p13	Signaling molecule	XY persistent Müllerian duct derivatives
DHH	12q13.1	Signaling molecule	Mutation: XY gonadal dysgenesis with neuropathy
ATRX	Xq13	Helicase	Feminized XY, mental retardation, α-thalassemia
WNT-4	1p35	Signaling molecule	Duplication: XY gondal dysgenesis Mutation: masculinized XX
Gdf9	5p11	Signaling molecule	Ovarian follicular failure
FOXL2	3q23	Transcription factor	Premature ovarian failure and eyelid defects

Source: Adapted from Corinne Cotinot et al., "Molecular Genetics of Sex Determination," *Seminars in Reproductive Medicine* 20 (2002): 158; Eric Vilain, "Genetics of Intersexuality," *Journal of Gay and Lesbian Psychotherapy* 10 (2006): 13; and Berenice B. Mendonca, Soharia Domenice, Ivo J. P. Arnhold, and Elaine M. F. Costa, "46,XY Disorders of Sex Development," *Clinical Endocrinology*, postprint, September 22, 2008, www3.interscience.wiley.com/cgi-bin/fulltext/121414874/PDFSTART.

Throughout the 1990s, then, Jost's testocentric model quickly unraveled under mounting evidence of the enormous complexity of mammalian sex determination, prompting the Australian molecular biologist Jennifer A. Marshall Graves to publish an article titled "Human Y Chromosome, Sex Determination, and Spermatogenesis — a Feminist View."[38] Although Richardson has argued that Graves as a scientific insider "normalized" the earlier feminist critique of the field, Graves never cites Fausto-Sterling's work or any social constructionist studies.[39] She apparently was less driven by feminist science studies than the internal collapse of what she humorously called the "macho" Y model under the growing weight of molecular biological findings. Graves hypothesizes instead that the Y chromosome is a "wimpy" chromosome, having lost many genes throughout mammalian evolution, and at the rate it is going will eventually vanish entirely in ten to a hundred million years. Sex determination will instead be taken over by the autosomal genes, as is now the case in mole voles (in which both sexes have a single X chromosome [in *Ellobius lutescens*] or XX [in *E. tancrei*]).

As the genetics of testicular development has become ever more complex in the past two decades, researchers have discovered it is intricately interwoven with the long-neglected genetics of ovarian development. A recent review article on ovarian development research opens by challenging the neo-Aristotelian perspective that has dominated the field: "Increasing evidence indicates that organogenesis of the ovary is not a passive process arising by default in the absence of the testis pathway."[40] Not surprisingly, ovarian development is proving to be as complex and polygenetic, with some genes promoting ovarian development and others suppressing testicular development. Finally, the discovery of XX individuals with testicular structures despite the absence of *SRY* has led one researcher to suggest that perhaps ovarian development is the active process and testicular development the passive default pathway — completely inverting the testocentric hypothesis.[41]

Gender and the Brain

The preceding discussion does not even begin to address the issues of gender identity and sexuality, which may also have some congenital, organic, and neurological foundations. Recent work in molecular genetics may shed new and controversial light on neuroanatomical sex differences. Phoebe Dewing and her colleagues in the lab of Eric Vilain, using microarray technology, have detected fifty-one out of twelve thousand genes active in the brain that are expressed at significantly different levels in male versus female mice at 10.5 days of embryogenesis (days postcoitum).[42] Since the nineteenth century, neuroanatomists have noted gross differences between male and female brains that were largely related to average differences in body size between men and women. But sex-specific differences in discrete brain regions have led to all sorts of speculation about their functional impact on cognition and behavior. The neuroscientist Simon LeVay made front-page news in 1991 with a very preliminary finding that (on average) there is a size difference in a region of the hypothalamus between homosexual and heterosexual men.[43] Whether associated with differences in gender or sexual orientation, these neuroanatomical differences were assumed by LeVay to be the result of in utero hormonal differences induced by the fetal gonads or the maternal hormonal milieu.[44]

What is striking, however, about Dewing's current research is that the differential gene expression was evident *before* the embryonic gonads had formed and could have produced androgens or estrogens. Contrary to LeVay's assumption of hormonal influences, Dewing's work argues that there are *genetically* induced sex differences in brain development. Again, the functional significance of these findings, if replicated, is up for speculation. Vilain, however, believes this murine research suggests genetic mechanisms of gender identity in the human brain with potential clinical value in assigning gender to neonates with ambiguous genitalia.[45] This line of research also potentially indicates a genetic basis for transsexualism and more broadly gender atypical behavior, if indeed there are genetic markers of neurological sex difference that more closely predict gender identity than even the sex chromosome karyotype. Whereas biologists (such as LeVay) are willing to conflate gender atypicality (the Victorian notion of "sexual inversion") and homosexuality, this research points to new genetic approaches to studying sexual orientation. Differential gene expression in *adult* male versus female brains will be another area of research used to explain sex differences in behavior: Dewing and her colleagues have presented data showing that *Sry* expression in rodents has an influence on the functioning of a specific, sexually dimorphic area of the rodent brain that affects movement.[46]

This neurogenetic research into sex differences is in its infancy and undoubtedly still fired by a conceptual ambitiousness inspired by limited data. However, if genital sex differentiation is any indicator, the biology of gender identity will most likely be even more complex in its molecular and hormonal mechanisms. Therefore only the most distorted and simplistic reading of the contemporary molecular biology of sex determination would suggest that it leads to a dichotomization of sex or gender. On the contrary, I find that this research deconstructs all prior Western scientific representations of sex, indicating instead the tremendous diversity of even the anatomical manifestations of sex. Extrapolating from this we would have to imagine that the diverse expressions of gender behavior and identity will prove even more complex and multideterminate in their biology, and regularly resist and challenge one gene–one trait models.

Microarray Gene Testing and Quantum Sex

In closing, let me return to Helen, who at just seventeen had to contend with huge anatomical, medical, familial, and social challenges. Although 46XY, her genital appearance was female, and there was never any question of gender reassignment simply to follow the dictates of her Y chromosome. Her kidney failure and transplant were one of the unfortunate defining features of DDS. The clitoral reduction, however, was medically unnecessary, and this type of "corrective" surgery has come under intense criticism thanks to ISNA activism.[47] The secrecy surrounding her diagnosis and treatment, while intended to protect her from the shock of her condition and any gender ambiguity, is probably misguided. She needs to understand her medical condition because she needs to remain under close medical attention her whole life, if only because of the kidney transplant. Correspondingly, over the past decade ISNA's position evolved toward greater collaboration with medical specialists to improve evaluation, education, and care of intersex patients, rather than a radical identity politics of demolishing the binary sex system in favor of a gender-free or gender-rainbow society.[48] This partnership with health care professionals is even more clearly enunciated as the mission of the new Accord Alliance that replaced ISNA in March 2008.

I would predict, however, that ISNA's treatment recommendations are likely to have increasing utility precisely as the binary sex system becomes ever more ragged at the edges. I am not suggesting that sex is not primarily bimodal—with two curves corresponding to two typical functional outcomes, male and female. Indeed, intersex conditions largely reinforce this, because in most cases where there are chromosomal or genetic anomalies the result is infertility or reduced fertility. The swiftly expanding research on the molecular genetics of gonadal development and neurological sex differences is certain to increase the overlapping tails of those male and female curves. This will particularly be true with DNA microarray technology.

Over the last decade of intense research fueled by the $3 billion Human Genome Project, the estimated total gene count for the human genome has shrunk to between twenty thousand and twenty-five thousand genes. Meanwhile, microarray testing has automated genetic testing such that over a half million probes of different genetic variations can be examined on a chip the size of a postage stamp for $250.[49] Accordingly, whole human genome testing is now a reality and will become ever more inexpensive.[50] It will become increasingly feasible to identify an individual's genetic variations or mutations of all genes or select genes. For example, prenatal genetic screening could be done for all thirty-five variants of the *WT1* gene as well as variants of all the other sex-determining genes known at the time, for an up-to-date sex genotype. Instead of simple sex chromosome data (usually XX or XY), parents would be presented with data on a dozen or, in the future, dozens of sex-related genes.

Leaping from this genotyping to an understanding of an individual's *phenotype*, however, will involve a complex statistical calculus. For example, there may be thirty-five variations of the *WT1* gene (*WT1* genotypes), each of which conveys certain statistical odds of particular anatomical and physiological outcomes (phenotypes). The specific phenotype—whether at birth or later in life—will also depend on the genotype of other genes (such as *SRY* and *DAX-1*) and their particular odds of producing certain phenotypes depending on the interaction of genes and tissues in embryogenesis or interactions with environmental factors later on in life. Sex determination will no longer be the simple matter of identifying a penis on ultrasound or XX/XY sex chromosome identification from an amniocentesis.

Molecular genetics is likely to require a shift from binary sex to quantum sex, with a dozen or more genes each conferring a small percentage likelihood of male or female sex that is still further dependent on micro- and macro-environmental interactions. As David Crews and colleagues point out: "Genes are not expressed in isolation any more than social behavior has meaning outside of society. Both are in dynamic flux with the immediate environment in which the gene/individual finds itself, which in turn establishes the timing, pattern, and conditions of expression."[51] Some biologists and science critics have long pointed out that nature and nurture are intimately intertwined. In the 1940s and 1950s, Barbara McClintock had been studying gene transposition as a mechanism by which the environment could alter genes in maize. Evelyn Fox Keller's biography of McClintock highlighted how she had to develop a new methodology and language to elaborate a dynamic model of interaction between the environment and the organism.[52] While it took several decades for McClintock's work to be rediscovered and accepted, research on sex determination afforded by intersex cases has prompted a dramatic shift within a decade. The hypothesis of a single testis-determining gene on the Y chromosome has quickly given way to a multigenetic network of gene regulation with time- and environment-sensitive factors.

The form of sex that emerges out of this quantum cloud of biological and environmental effects is at once culturally defined and personally discovered.

Helen's experience of her sex, gender, and sexuality is intimately tied to her sense of her body — to what is evident on the surface, to what she understands to be her internal anatomy, to her lost genital and gonadal flesh, and to her genetic makeup. At seventeen she was probably not conscious of the historical and cultural constructions of gender, intersexes, and sexuality that have influenced what happened to her body, yet she will have to construct for herself a new experience of her body that allows for sexual intimacy, erotic pleasure, and a fulfilling relationship with women, men, or both. The new molecular genetics of sex is likely to pose similar ontological and existential challenges to an increasing number of people with medical issues less life threatening than Helen's. The new DSD terminology tends to narrow the sphere of intersex to individuals with clear pathology of the reproductive system. This is a practical taxonomic move for focusing on the problem of early genital corrective surgery. I would predict, however, that the complex new molecular genetics of sex — along with widespread genetic testing — will widen the sphere or, at least, further blur the boundaries of what is intersex. Thus the medical and sociopolitical challenge of intersexuality will hopefully prompt a broader and more complex understanding of sex/gender/sexuality as a biological, psychological, and cultural phenomenon that is rich, diverse, and indefinitely complex, resistant to all simplistic reductionism, whether biological or discursive.

Notes

1. Cheryl Chase, letter to the editor, *Sciences*, July – August 1993, 3.
2. A new nomenclature using the term *DSD* was hammered out by a consensus group of pediatric endocrinologists, urologists, and geneticists, with much support from ISNA; see Peter A. Lee et al., "Summary of Consensus Statement on Intersex Disorders and Their Management," *Pediatrics* 118 (2006): 753–57; Alice Dreger et al., "Changing the Nomenclature/Taxonomy for Intersex: A Scientific and Clinical Rationale," *Journal of Pediatric Endocrinology* 18 (2005): 729–33; Eric Vilain et al., "We Used to Call Them Hermaphrodites," *Genetics in Medicine* 9 (2007): 65–66. This change represents ISNA's decisive move to reconstruct intersex as a medical matter and not one of cultural identity politics. In this essay I continue to use *intersex* because of its familiarity and to highlight its cultural messiness rather than sanitize it with a medicalizing acronym. The DSD acronym is predictably controversial among some intersex activists committed to a radical depathologization of intersex and a critique of the "dogmatic fundamentalism inherent in the current binary construct of sex and gender" (Organisation Intersex International, "DSD — Is There Really a Consensus?" www.intersexualite.org/Disorders_of_Sex_Development.html [accessed July 29, 2008]). The intersex activist Emi Koyama offers a pragmatic acceptance of the

DSD term in the context of disability studies and a politics of depathologizing pathology itself ("From 'Intersex' to 'DSD': Toward a Queer Disability Politics of Gender" [2006], www.intersexinitiative.org/articles/intersextodsd.html).

3. John Colapinto, *As Nature Made Him: The Boy Who Was Raised as a Girl* (New York: HarperCollins, 2000); Milton Diamond and H. Keith Sigmundson, "Sex Reassignment at Birth: Long-Term Review and Clinical Implications," *Archives of Pediatric and Adolescent Medicine* 151 (1997): 298–304.

4. Bernice L. Hausman, *Changing Sex: Transsexualism, Technology, and the Idea of Gender* (Durham, NC: Duke University Press, 1995), 95.

5. Natalie Angier, "Sexual Identity Not Pliable After All, Report Says," *New York Times*, March 14, 1997.

6. "Anatomy *Is* Destiny," *New York Post*, March 17, 1997.

7. Anne Fausto-Sterling, "How Many Sexes Are There?" *New York Times*, March 12, 1993.

8. Suzanne J. Kessler, *Lessons from the Intersexed* (New Brunswick, NJ: Rutgers University Press, 1998), 132.

9. Judith Butler, "Doing Justice to Someone: Sex Reassignment and Allegories of Transsexuality," *GLQ* 7 (2001): 621–36. Milton Diamond rebuts her in "Biased-Interaction Theory of Psychosexual Development: 'How Does One Know If One Is Male or Female?'" *Sex Roles* 55 (2006): 589–600.

10. C. E. M. van Beijsterveldt, James J. Hudziak, and Dorret I. Boomsma, "Genetic and Environmental Influences on Cross-Gender Behavior and Relation to Behavior Problems: A Study of Dutch Twins at Ages 7 and 10 Years," *Archives of Sexual Behavior* 35 (2006): 647–58.

11. Nicholas Wade, "Pas de Deux of Sexuality Is Written in the Genes," *New York Times*, April 10, 2007.

12. S. J. McTaggart et al. "Clinical Spectrum of Denys-Drash and Frasier Syndrome," *Pediatric Nephrology* 16 (2001): 335–39.

13. A note on abbreviation and typesetting conventions in molecular genetics: abbreviations of gene names are italicized. The protein for which the gene codes is designated in nonitalics. For example, the *WT1* gene codes for WT1 protein. Human genes are abbreviated in capitals, while in other animals only the first letter of the gene name is capitalized—for example, *WT1* in humans, *Wt1* in mice.

14. Anwar Hossain and Grady F. Saunders, "The Human Sex-Determining Gene *SRY* Is a Direct Target of *WT1*," *Journal of Biological Chemistry* 276 (2001): 16817–23; Jürgen Klattig et al., "Wilms' Tumor Protein Wt1 Is an Activator of the Anti-Müllerian Hormone Receptor Gene *Amhr2*," *Molecular and Cellular Biology* 27 (2007): 4355–64.

15. A similar condition, Frasier syndrome (characterized by 46XY karyotype, normal female genitalia, streak gonads, and later renal disease but no tumor), was found to

be associated with a different set of mutations in *WT1* (A. Koziell et al., "Frasier Syndrome: Part of the Denys-Drash Continuum or Simply a *WT1* Gene-Associated Disorder of Intersex and Nephropathy?" *Clinical Endocrinology* 52 [2000]: 519–24).

16. R. F. Mueller, "The Denys-Drash Syndrome," *Journal of Medical Genetics* 31 (1994): 471–77.

17. Thomas Laqueur, *Making Sex: Body and Gender from the Greeks to Freud* (Cambridge, MA: Harvard University Press, 1990).

18. James Kiernan, "Sexual Perversion," *Detroit Lancet* 7 (1884): 481–84.

19. The paired Müllerian (or paramesonephric) ducts develop into the female internal reproductive organs — fallopian tubes, uterus, cervix, and upper two-thirds of the vagina. The lower third of the vagina develops from the invagination of the urogenital sinus on the external surface of the groin. Failure of the lower part of the paired ducts to fuse leads to a bicornuate (two-horned) uterus. In males the Müllerian ducts usually degenerate because of testicular secretion of anti-Müllerian hormone (AMH), leaving behind an appendix testis on each side. The AMH gene is at locus 19p13.3 — also not on the sex chromosomes. The paired Wolffian (or mesonephric) ducts usually develop with the stimulation of testosterone into the male reproductive tract connecting the testes to the exterior — rete testis, epididymis, vas deferens, seminal vesicle, and central zone of the prostate. The peripheral and transitional zones of the prostate develop from the urogenital sinus. Usually in females the Wolffian duct degenerates, leaving behind a remnant, the Gartner duct.

20. At thirty-two days postconception in humans the primordial germ cells begin to differentiate. At fifty-five to sixty days anti-Müllerian hormone begins to be secreted and the Müllerian duct begins to regress in males. At nine weeks testosterone is produced in males, and there is masculinization of the urogenital sinus and external genitalia. At ten weeks the Wolffian ducts regress in females.

21. Stephen G. Brush, "Nettie M. Stevens and the Discovery of Sex Determination by Chromosomes," *Isis* 69 (1978): 165; Jane Maienschein, "What Determines Sex? A Study of Converging Approaches, 1880–1916," *Isis* 75 (1984): 456–80.

22. H. Henking, "Untersuchungen über die ersten Entwicklungvorgänge in der Eiern der Insekten II: Über Spermatogenese und deren Beziehung zur Eientwicklung bei *Pyrrhocoris apterus*" ("Investigations into the Early Developments of Insect Eggs II: Concerning Spermatogenesis and Its Relationship to Egg Development in *Pyrrhocoris apteris*"), *Zeitschrift für wissenschaftliche Zoologie* 51 (1891): 685–736.

23. C. E. McClung, "The Accessory Chromosome — Sex Determinant?" *Biological Bulletin* 3 (1902): 72.

24. Nettie M. Stevens, *Studies in Spermatogenesis with Especial Reference to the "Accessory Chromosome"* (Washington, DC: Carnegie Institution, 1905).

25. Edmund B. Wilson, "Studies on Chromosomes I: The Behavior of the Idiochromosomes in *Hemiptera*," *Journal of Experimental Zoology* 2 (1905): 371–405.

26. Derek Chadwick and Jamie Goode, eds., *The Genetics and Biology of Sex Determination* (New York: Wiley, 2002).

27. Alfred Jost, "Recherches sur la différenciation sexuelle de l'embryon de lapin III: Rôle des gonades foetales dans la différentiation sexuelle somatique" ("Research into the Sexual Differentiation of the Rabbit Embryo III: The Role of Fetal Gonads in Somatic Sexual Differentiation"), *Archives d'Anatomie Microscopique et de Morphologie Expérimentale* 36 (1947): 271–315.

28. Once testes begin to develop they produce Müllerian inhibiting substance, which inhibits the further development of Fallopian tubes and uterus, and the testes secrete testosterone, which stimulates development of male internal genitalia and masculinization of the external genitalia.

29. Aristotle, *Generation of Animals*, trans. A. L. Peck (Cambridge, MA: Harvard University Press, 1942), 716a5.

30. See also Joan Cadden, *Meanings of Sex Difference in the Middle Ages: Medicine, Science, and Culture* (New York: Cambridge University Press, 1993).

31. Sarah S. Richardson, "When Gender Criticism Becomes Standard Scientific Practice: The Case of Sex Determination Genetics," in *Gendered Innovations in Science and Engineering*, ed. Londa Schiebinger (Stanford: Stanford University Press, 2008), 22–42. Eicher and Washburn in a review of mouse sex determination research pointed out that researchers represent testis determination as an active gene-directed event, while the induction of the ovary is a default passive event. This leads to the complete neglect of genetic research on ovarian tissue development, which they point out must be as active and genetically directed as any tissue development ("Genetic Control of Primary Sex Determination in Mice," *Annual Review of Genetics* 20 [1986]: 328). Fausto-Sterling in her "Life in the XY Corral" (*Women's Studies International Forum* 12 [1989]: 319–31) cited Eicher and Washburn in a more pointedly feminist critique of the female passivity ideology underlying David Page's 1987 identification — which ultimately proved erroneous — of a testis-determining gene.

32. Philippe Berta et al., "Genetic Evidence Equating *SRY* and the Testis-Determining Factor," *Nature* 348 (1990): 448–50; Ralf J. Jäger et al., "A Human XY Female with a Frame Shift Mutation in the Candidate Testis-Determining Gene *SRY*," *Nature* 348 (1990): 452–54; Christopher M. Haqq and Patricia K. Donahoe, "Regulation of Sexual Dimorphism in Mammals," *Physiological Reviews* 78 (1998): 1–33.

33. Nelson B. Phillips et al., "SRY and Human Sex Determination: The Basic Tail of the HMG Box Functions as a Kinetic Clamp to Augment DNA Bending," *Journal of Molecular Biology* 358 (2006): 172–92.

34. Hossain and Saunders, "Human Sex-Determining Gene *SRY*."

35. Paul D. Waters, Mary C. Wallis, and Jennifer A. Marshall Graves, "Mammalian Sex — Origin and Evolution of the Y Chromosome and *SRY*," *Seminars in Cell and Developmental Biology* 18 (2007): 389–400.

36. Nelly Oudshoorn, "On the Making of Sex Hormones: Research Materials and the Production of Knowledge," *Social Studies of Science* 20 (1990): 5–33.

37. Waters et al., "Mammalian Sex."

38. Jennifer A. Marshall Graves, "Human Y Chromosome, Sex Determination, and Spermatogenesis—a Feminist View," *Biology of Reproduction* 63 (2000): 667–76.

39. Richardson, "When Gender Criticism Becomes Standard Scientific Practice."

40. Humphrey Hung-Chang Yao, "The Pathway to Femaleness: Current Knowledge on Embryonic Development of the Ovary," *Molecular and Cellular Endocrinology* 230 (2005): 87.

41. Yao, "Pathway to Femaleness," 91.

42. Phoebe Dewing et al., "Sexually Dimorphic Gene Expression in Mouse Brain Precedes Gonadal Differentiation," *Molecular Brain Research* 118 (2003): 82–90.

43. Simon LeVay, "A Difference in Hypothalamic Structure between Heterosexual and Homosexual Men," *Science* 253 (1991): 1034–37.

44. For contrasting accounts, see G. Dörner et al., "Gene- and Environment-Dependent Neuroendocrine Etiogenesis of Homosexuality and Transsexualism," *Experimental and Clinical Endocrinology* 98 (1991): 141–50; and Roger A. Gorski, "Sexual Differentiation of the Endocrine Brain and Its Control," in *Brain Endocrinology*, ed. Marcella Motta (New York: Raven, 1991), 71–104.

45. Carina Dennis, "The Most Important Sexual Organ," *Nature* 427 (2004): 390–92.

46. Phoebe Dewing et al., "Direct Regulation of Adult Brain Function by the Male-Specific Factor SRY," *Current Biology* 16 (2006): 415–20.

47. Cheryl Chase, "Hermaphrodites with Attitude: Mapping the Emergence of Intersex Political Activism," *GLQ* 4 (1998): 189–211.

48. See ISNA's Web site promoting the new DSD terminology and treatment guidelines: www.dsdguidelines.org.

49. This Genome-Wide Human SNP Array 5.0 is produced by Affymetrix: www.affymetrix.com/products/arrays/specific/genome_wide/genome_wide_snp_5.affx (accessed July 29, 2008).

50. In May 2007 the Baylor College of Medicine and gene-testing technology company 454 Life Sciences announced the sequencing of a complete human genome, that of DNA codiscoverer James Watson: www.454.com/watson (accessed July 29, 2008).

51. David Crews et al., "From Gene Networks Underlying Sex Determination and Gonadal Differentiation to the Development of Neural Networks Regulating Sociosexual Behavior," *Brain Research* 1126 (2006): 109.

52. Evelyn Fox Keller, *A Feeling for the Organism: The Life and Work of Barbara McClintock* (San Francisco: Freeman, 1983).

WHAT CAN QUEER THEORY DO FOR INTERSEX?

Iain Morland

The Time of the Touch

*T*o queers and nonqueers alike the visceral immediacy of the sexual touch might appear to be self-evident; contact between a lover's body and one's own is typically coincident with the mutual sensation of such contact. Even an unwelcome sexual advance is recognizable by its tactile impression—for instance, the brush of a hand from which one immediately recoils. In short, touching and feeling happen live.

My starting point in this essay is that when the nerves in one's genitalia have been damaged by surgery, the time of the touch changes. For example, one sees a lover's hand touching one's genitalia, but one does not feel it. Hence the apparently real time of sexual experience—in which, as Sarah E. Chinn claims in an essay about queer touching, "our bodies feel and are felt outside solely visual perception"—turns into the contemplative voyeurism of pornography.[1] Touching happens, but it is seen rather than sensed, and in Chinn's opinion vision "is virtually useless when it comes to figuring out and describing the experience of sexual pleasure" (182). I know from direct personal experience that this is profoundly disorienting; when genitalia are insensate, the time of the touch stretches infinitely away from the moment of physical contact. Perhaps one can recall how it felt to be touched prior to genital surgery, or imagine how it might feel if sensation were to return in the future to one's genitalia—either way, touching and feeling are riven, too late or too early to coincide.

Consider in this regard a 1996 letter to the influential *Journal of Urology*, in which the founder of the Intersex Society of North America (ISNA), Cheryl Chase, described some of the postsurgical problems reported by society members.

GLQ 15:2
DOI 10.1215/10642684-2008-139
© 2009 by Duke University Press

Several had experienced either diminished or extinguished genital sensation following surgery for intersex. One member whose clitoris was reduced in childhood found orgasm "so difficult to reach and so rarely attained" that she regarded her "sexual function as being destroyed."[2] Disturbingly, another felt "intense genital pain" following sexual stimulation (1,140). More recently, a study by a London-based medical team evaluated clitoral sensation in six intersex women whose clitorises had been surgically reduced. The study was innovative because it used not merely a sexual satisfaction questionnaire but also electronic devices to measure clitoral sensitivity to temperature and vibration. These provided gradually increasing stimuli until participants pressed a button to register sensation. It was the first time that such "objective sensory testing" had been performed on individuals with a history of genital surgery.[3] Postsurgical clitoral sensation in the six women was found to be "profoundly abnormal" (138). All had atypical results for the sensation of cold, and five participants had abnormal results for the sensation of warmth and vibration. In response to the questionnaire four women said they had problems achieving orgasm. Worryingly, this was not the legacy of outdated surgical techniques: the authors of the study cautioned that "there is currently no justification for the optimism that modern surgical techniques are better for preserving clitoral sensation than previous operations" (138). The caution was an implicit rejoinder to the criticism by earlier clinicians that the individuals discussed in Chase's letter had not benefited from "changes in the surgical approach" since the mid-1970s.[4] Even if scholars in the theoretical humanities might query the London team's claim to objectivity, it's still pragmatically useful in making their study authoritative to other doctors, as well as in substantiating Chase's letter.

What kinds of critiques of genital surgery does queer theory enable or substantiate? In this essay I investigate what queer theory can do for intersex bodies that have been desensitized by genital surgery. Of course, surgery for intersex does not wholly desensitize entire bodies, but in what follows I refer often to desensitized postsurgical *bodies* rather than merely genitalia for three reasons. The first reason isn't specific to intersex: any experience of surgery extends beyond the scalpel's cut. Even anesthesia can cause postoperative nausea and vomiting.[5] The second and third reasons are more specific. Nerve damage can alter the perception and tactility of areas other than those where cutting has been performed.[6] Finally, surgery for intersex does not operate solely on exterior genitalia; it can also change, reposition, or remove internal structures, for instance by creating a vagina from a segment of colon.[7] In short, the whole body undergoes surgery, and the experience of surgery is lived by the body as a whole, even if the body is cut in only a small area—hence one ISNA member's claim that clitoral surgery had destroyed "sexual function" in general. My aim, then, is not to use queer theory to undo the diverse bodily effects of genital surgery. Rather, I evaluate whether a critique of surgery's effects is possible from a queer theoretical perspective on the body.

To this end I make four key claims, beginning with my reservations about queer discourses of pleasure and shame. My first claim is that the desensitized postsurgical body cannot be accounted for by a queer discourse in which sexual pleasure is a form of hedonistic activism. Consequently, I seek to follow Robert Jensen's recommendation that our task as sexual dissidents "is not necessarily imagining new ways of touching but always being attentive to the ethics and politics of the touch."[8] In other words, a queer reaction to the problems of intersex surgery cannot be simply the advocacy of more and better sex, because that's precisely what intersex surgery can make at best pointless and at worst impossible. Instead we must proceed with careful awareness of how previous touches on intersexed bodies, such as the desensitizing touch of the surgeon, change those bodies and thereby constrain the possibilities for queer critique. My second claim is that a queer discourse of shame enables a critical engagement with the surgical creation of atypically sensate bodies. As Sara Ahmed has commented, an ethics of touch is not just about touching others but about sensitivity to the way others have already been touched and affected—in this instance how bodies obdurately remember the shameful touch of surgery, no matter how desperately we may wish to brush its effects away.[9] Nevertheless I do not wish to suggest that queer critics need simply to choose between theorizing intersex in terms of either pleasure or shame. There is really no such opposition. My third key claim, then, is that queerness is characterized by the sensory interrelation of pleasure and shame, for as David M. Halperin puts it, "the genius of gay sex—and not only *gay* sex—lies precisely in its ability to transmute otherwise unpleasant experiences of social degradation into experiences of pleasure."[10] If there exists "a queer ethic of dignity in shame," in Michael Warner's words, my interest lies not in revealing shame to be a kind of pleasure or vice versa.[11] I am interested instead in the fact that shame and pleasure are both queer *sensations*; I argue that queer theory's assumption of a sensorial basis to cultural critique flounders when confronted with the desensitized intersex body. In the light of this, my fourth and final claim is that if queer theory is figured as a kind of reaching—but not necessarily touching—then it can be of greater use in accounting for the problematic effects of intersex surgery. Thus the reach is queerer than the touch, for it is a recognition that, as Lee Edelman has written, "queer theory can only remain a desire, and like desire it depends for its energy, for its continuing power to grip us, on the impossibility of knowing its boundaries, of knowing its coherence as a state."[12] In my opinion, desire is what queer theory and the postsurgical intersex body have in common. But for this reason I think Edelman's idea of "gripping" isn't quite right; I would say that desire *reaches* through queer and intersex bodies alike. I argue in closing that desire's reach confounds the surgical project of touching atypical bodies in order to make them sexually normal.

Queer Pleasures

Queer theory would appear to facilitate a critique of diminished sexual pleasure following intersex surgery. This is because queer theory, together with related strands of third-wave feminism, is the academic discourse that has had the most to say about the cultural significance and experience of human sexual pleasure: it is a "vision of social production that engages the libidinal," in Edelman's words (344). Unlike the emphasis within second-wave feminism on gender, and specifically in "antisex" feminism on sexual pleasure as a ruse of gender oppression, queer theory has taken the sexual and its pleasures as central objects of study. In her groundbreaking 1979 essay "A Secret Side of Lesbian Sexuality," Pat Califia drew a contrast between the "pleasure" of sadomasochism and "real slavery or exploitation."[13] The contrast would become a central issue for both third-wave feminism and queer theory. Significantly, Califia described as "ephemeral" sadomasochism's pleasures, unlike "economic control or forced reproduction" (166). The opposition here was not only between pleasure and displeasure but also between the felt immediacy of sexual activities and the protracted historicity of institutionalized heterosexuality. In this way sadomasochism is "time-consuming and absorbing," in Califia's words (166), paradoxically because its pleasures are transitory — a series of present moments that viscerally envelop the sexual subject, rather than a history of sexuality of which the regulated sexual subject is the effect. By equating sadomasochism with a unique time of pleasure, Califia was able to articulate a feminism that was distinctively neither heterosexual nor antisex. During the 1980s and 1990s such countercultural possibilities of sexual pleasure would be analyzed and celebrated by third-wave feminism and in turn queer theory. Of course other queer theories would also emerge — such as those centered upon shame, loss, drag, and temporality, on which I'll draw later in this article — but I want to discuss pleasure first because the diminution of pleasure seems to be the defining problem with genital desensitization. If queer theory can tell us why pleasure is valuable, then it follows that a queer discourse of pleasure can pinpoint why the diminution of pleasure makes genital desensitization wrong.

The central theme of Califia's account — sexual pleasure as converse to sexuality's institutional formations — has shaped the interface between queer theory and intersex. An important axiom of queer theory has been that sex acts can be pleasurable even if — or perhaps because — they occur outside mainstream norms. This is demonstrated by Califia's contrast between subcultural sadomasochism and institutionalized heterosexuality. Just as a queer discourse of pleasure prioritizes transient sexual activities over stable gender identities, so too has intersex activism emphasized healthy sexual functioning as an alternative to reforming gender categories.[14] Thus intersex activism and much queer theory have in common the project of "opening up a new space for the subject of desire," as one commentator on queer theory has described.[15] In this regard both discourses address a subject for whom sexuality functions without adherence to mainstream norms. Now this does not mean that individuals with intersex anatomies necessarily have queer desires; rather, several intersex activists and scholars have called intersex bodies queer in their deviation from norms of embodiment.[16] Queer theory and intersex activism converge on the belief that such deviation is not an obstacle to sexual pleasure, contrary to what medicine has traditionally assumed. A queer discourse of pleasure, then, is useful in critiquing the normalizing use of genital surgery — for instance, when clinicians have evaluated vaginal surgery in terms of whether "adequate intercourse . . . defined as successful vaginal penetration" is possible postoperatively, or when they have reported in childhood surgical outcome studies on whether patients have subsequently entered into heterosexual marriages.[17] As Morgan Holmes complains, "When parents sign consent forms, allowing doctors to remove the erotogenic tissue of their children, they are willingly following a heterosexist requirement that humans live as either male or female."[18] The sacrifice of sensation ("erotogenic tissue") to the norm ("heterosexist requirement") is opposed by Holmes. Nevertheless, to enjoy sexual pleasure outside mainstream norms is not the same as to enjoy sexual pleasure in the absence of all constraints; I return to this caveat shortly.

Another queer axiom presciently thematized in Califia's essay is less a simple rejection of heterosexuality than a deployment of pleasure to resist sexuality's institutionalized forms, of which mainstream heterosexuality is one formation among others. For example, Douglas Crimp has eschewed the perceived institutionalism of gay marriage in favor of the "life-affirming and pleasure-filled world" of homosexual subculture.[19] More than a critique of gender identity, queer theory has enabled an understanding and experience of sex acts as signifiers of pleasure, not signifiers of sexual identity. Sex acts can therefore be resignified within a queer discourse of pleasure, much as the word *queer* has itself undergone countercultural reclamation and revision.[20] Such resignification encompasses acts commonly considered heterosexual, for as Califia has argued, "a belief in sex differences and a dependence on them for sexual pleasure is the most common perversion."[21] In this view heterosexual sex is not motivated by heterosexual identity; it is merely one perversion among many, pursued for pleasure while overlaid by privilege. When heterosexual sex is cast as a pleasure like any other, the institutionalized privileges of heterosexuality are highlighted as unwarranted. The surgical sacrifice of genital sensation to heterosexuality is therefore not only a curtailment of individual pleasure, but also a fundamental misrecognition of the individual as the institution. For the former, heterosexual sex is a source of pleasure; in the latter, heterosexual identity is a source of privilege. Consequently, to create a heterosexual individual through desensitizing genital surgery is a contradiction in terms.

The work of Michel Foucault has been instrumental in the politics of resignification. Despite some leftist resistance to the first volume of Foucault's *History of Sexuality* for its incongruous coupling of a sweeping account of sex and power with an obtusely brisk discussion of how such power can be resisted, Halperin argues that "lesbian and gay militants" have been perhaps the most receptive audience for Foucault's thought.[22] This includes such activists as the AIDS Coalition to Unleash Power, because as Halperin notes, "the public response to AIDS" in the United States in the 1980s perfectly illustrated "the mutual imbrication of power and knowledge" concerning sex that Foucault analyzed—for example, the "endless relays between expert discourse and institutional authority . . . and local struggles for survival and resistance" (27). Consequently, Halperin envisages AIDS activism as accelerating "a multiplication of the sites of political contestation beyond such traditional arenas as the electoral process" to "ultimately the public and the private administration of the body and its pleasures." This strategy, which includes critical interventions into medical practice, is Foucauldian to the extent that volume 1 of *The History of Sexuality* "had already treated the body as a site of political struggle" (28). There Foucault asserted that sexuality is "organized by power in its grip on bodies and their materiality, their forces, energies, sensations, and pleasures," and famously recommended that "the grips of power" should be resisted by "bodies and pleasures."[23] Foucault argued, in other words, for bodily pleasure as a way to resist power.

Within queer theory there have emerged two distinct views on the relation between bodies and pleasures. According to one view, pleasure is obtained exclusively or most effectively through use of the genitalia. Hence for Queer Nation, in the words of Lauren Berlant, genitalia were "not just organs of erotic thanksgiving, but weapons of pleasure against their own oppression."[24] What makes such genital terrorism queer is the combination of genitalia in a given sex act; queer sex for that reason can shock heterosexual culture. This is what Tim Dean has called queer theory's "insistence on the specificity of genital contact as the basis for all political work."[25] According to the other view of the relation between bodies and pleasures, queer pleasure is characterized by a focus not on genitalia but on the body as a whole. For example, according to Mark Blasius, homosexual relations become queer when they use "every part of the body as a sexual instrument in order to achieve the greatest intensification of pleasure possible."[26] The result is what Halperin called "a multiplication of the sites of political contestation" on the level of the body. In this distinctly Foucauldian view, queer sex can effect cultural change through its stylized attention to reciprocal "erotic pleasure," quite aside from the genital morphologies of its participants.[27] The latter view is notable also for the continuity that it signals between queer theory and third-wave feminism, in which heterosexual relations are often acceptable so long as they are similarly "nongenitally organized."[28] For writers like Califia, sadomasochism is paradigmatic of such relations.

In both views, the valorization of pleasure in queer subcultures can be a source of pride. But the capacity of the postsurgical body to participate in such subcultures is unclear. Chase, anorgasmic after genital surgery for intersex, has criticized "sex radicals and activists" who claim that she is having "vaginal" or "full-body" orgasms despite her insistence to the contrary. Understandably, Chase finds highly patronizing their assumption that she will "learn how to orgasm."[29] A queer theory focused on pleasure alone, whether exclusively genital or diffusely "full-body," risks characterizing postsurgical intersex bodies as irrevocably impoverished.[30] Correspondingly, a queer critique of intersex treatment, advanced on the grounds that presurgical intersex bodies are queer in their physical sexual dissidence, may cast postsurgical intersex bodies as *less* queer—or not queer at all. To clarify this assertion, I don't mean that after surgery intersex bodies are less queer because surgery successfully eliminates a queer presurgical anatomy. Rather, I am making a point about physiological functioning: the postsurgical body, irrespective of the degree to which it still looks sexually ambiguous, may be less amenable to queer analysis and political participation because of its diminished capacity for sexual pleasure.

Queer Shame

Readers might object that my discussion in the previous section presumed sex between bodies that *haven't* had intersex surgery to be straightforwardly pleasurable, and further that the presence of pleasure is inversely proportional to pleasure's absence. But as I discuss now, not all queer discourse has conceived of sex in this way, so different queer theories of the postsurgical intersex body are possible.

One's conception of sexual pleasure determines one's conception of desensitizing genital surgery as injurious. Although the discourses of pleasure discussed above enable a queer critique of surgery on the grounds that the loss of sexual pleasure is bad, such criticism depends on the conception of sexual pleasure as something that can be lost. Likewise, within those queer discourses the diminution of sexual pleasure is objectionable in part because it raises the possibility of sexual pleasure's extinction. Now if sex is purely pleasurable, and pleasure is the opposite of no pleasure, then it is indeed possible to lose the capacity for, and hence the experience of, sexual pleasure. However, if sex is something more or other than pleasurable, then pleasure's presence and absence are not necessarily opposed, and accordingly the idea of lost sexual pleasure is far less straightforward. While some queer theory, in line with much gay pride discourse, has measured the effects of homophobia by the extent to which homophobia limits subcultural sexual pleasures, other queer theorizations of sex have been more ambivalent. Specifically, they have queried the Foucauldian conception of sex as a matter of bodies and pleasures, for as Sally Munt argues, however "strategically essential" pride in sexual dissidence may be, "the presence of shame has been repressed in the discourse of homosexual rights in an unhelpful way, and in order to gain greater agency, we must learn to revisit its ambivalent effects."[31] In light of Munt's claim I want to evaluate what queer attention to shame, rather than to pleasure, might do for intersex.

Within queer theory the most well-known account of sex — and not merely queer sex — as an experience more ambivalent than pleasurable was given by Leo Bersani in his 1987 essay "Is the Rectum a Grave?" The essay's provocative title reflects the fact that Bersani was writing in reaction to the AIDS crisis. Although, as I've shown, Halperin has presented a Foucauldian turn to bodies and pleasures as resistant to those structures of power and knowledge that conflated homosexuality with social collapse and death, Bersani's incendiary response to the same epidemic was to query whether homosexuality is, after all, in some way antithetical to the social as it has been defined in mainstream Western culture. The big secret about sex, Bersani advances, is that "most people don't like it" — which is to say neither that people don't think about sex a lot, nor that people don't want to have a lot of sex.[32] Instead, Bersani's point is that sex is not as pleasurable as it might seem to us while we're daydreaming about it. When we actually have sex, Bersani claims, we are no longer self-contained subjects enjoying an easily quantifiable experience of pleasure that we have contemplated beforehand. Quite the reverse: for Bersani, sex is an experience of radical dissolution that he calls "self-shattering" (222). Sexuality is therefore "socially dysfunctional," in Bersani's words, not because it can sometimes be the genital terrorism of Queer Nation but because it always undoes "the supposed relationality or community of the couple (which depends on selfhood)," as a commentator on Bersani's essay puts it.[33] Regardless of the number of participants, sex is a profoundly solipsistic experience. So in Bersani's account the passive "suicidal ecstasy" of the gay bottom exemplifies a general theory of sex as nonrelational.[34] This has subsequently become known as the "antisocial thesis" in queer theory.[35]

The antisocial account of sex puts in question the apparently self-evident badness of desensitizing genital surgery. If sex isn't pleasurable anyway, then the diminution or loss of sexual pleasure is at least a misnomer and perhaps also a contradiction. It is a misnomer if something other than pleasure — a shattering — is lost to postsurgical sex; it is a contradiction if a loss of pleasure — again, a shattering — characterizes sex in general. An obvious way to resolve this conundrum would be to say simply that shattering is just another name for pleasure, which is what Bersani argues elsewhere about the apparent pain of masochism: we might then say that self-shattering describes only the transformation of "stimuli generally associated with the production of pain into stimuli that set off intense processes identified as pleasurable," as Bersani comments on masochism.[36] But rather than try to sanitize shattering by defending it as a "pleasurable debasement," the antisocial thesis in queer theory has developed into a complex discourse about negativity, futurity, and — most significantly for my argument — shame.[37] In short, the antisocial character of sex — debasing, disintegrating, demeaning — makes sex shameful. Queer subcultures, it has been argued, have a distinctive relationship to such shame; if sex for both queers and nonqueers is a kind of shattering, then what distinguishes queer subcultures isn't the performance of certain sex acts (genital terrorism, whole-body sadomasochism, or anything else) but a particular attitude toward the antisocial experience of sex. In queer subcultures, according to Warner, "one doesn't pretend to be *above* the indignity of sex," since "we're all in it together."[38] In this way, an "acknowledgement of all that is most abject and least reputable in oneself" — namely, the solipsistic evacuation described by Bersani — perversely enables "the special kind of sociability that holds queer culture together" (35). That is, queer subcultures are characterized by the recognition that sex is antisocial.

Nonetheless, if sex is really as shamefully antisocial as Bersani describes, one has to wonder why people have sex at all. I'm not raising this issue in order to retreat from Bersani's claim to a version of queer sex that is cuddly hand-holding; his claim is important and deserves interrogation. Even though Bersani aims to "desexualize the erotic" by casting it as antisocial, his account remains resolutely sexualized in its valorization of gay anal penetration as the exemplary "intensification or . . . mode of revelation of an always-already shattering self," as Kathryn Bond Stockton writes in her book about shame.[39] As a consequence, there is a circularity in Bersani's argument. He explains, through reference to sex, why "most people don't like sex," as if most people don't like it because they've had it, but didn't like the way in which it shattered them. This doesn't account for those people who haven't had sex, can't have it, or don't want to have it in the first place. Yet I think those people may be no less queer. A critique of queer theory by Heather Love is useful on this point. Love has argued that "queer desire is often figured as . . . excessive, dissonant desire. But it would also make sense to understand queerness as an absence of or aversion to sex."[40] Both types of queerness presented by Love are possible on the basis of the antisocial thesis, but much queer theory has alighted on the first (queerness as an excessive embrace of shameful shattering) while failing to investigate the second (queerness as a rejection of, or withdrawal from, sex). The absence of sex, as Love admits, is "not very sexy," and for that reason has received little critical attention (175n22). But if queer theory is to do anything for intersex, it needs to theorize the ways in which postsurgical bodies may be asexual, and even downright unsexy to some people — including sometimes those who dwell in such bodies. The shattering experience of sex might be shameful — the antisocial thesis teaches us that much — but not having sex, or having sex without shattering, can be shameful, too.

In queer discourse the body of the stone butch is sometimes presented as the somatic personalization of the absence of or aversion to sex described by Love. Traditionally, a stone butch makes love to her femme partner but refuses to be touched in return.[41] In a groundbreaking essay on the subject, Judith Halberstam has criticized any simplistic conception of stone butch "impenetrability" as a "closed" sexuality (63, 68). In an argument that may seem equivalent to Chase's rejection of claims that she will learn how to orgasm, Halberstam contests the representation of stoneness as "a wall that has been built up and could come down with the right femme" (68).

Despite the stone butch body's closure to genital penetration, Halberstam suggests that it is "open to rubbing or friction," and in this regard "butch untouchability multiplies the possibilities of touch," as one commentator on Halberstam notes.[42] To be stone, then, is "a courageous and imaginative way of dealing with the contradictory demands and impulses of being a butch in a woman's body,"

according to Halberstam (69). But for this very reason there are two critical differences between stone butch and intersex. The former is a "sexual identity" (71),
whereas the latter is an anatomy. I agree with Ellen K. Feder, writing elsewhere in
this journal issue, that there are not "intersex individuals" in the same way that
there are "homosexual individuals."[43] Further, because the queerness of the stone
butch lies not in sexual "closure" but in the performance and reception of certain
kinds of touching, the stone butch body is still a tactile body. It is therefore vital to
examine whether there is a similar place for the postsurgical intersex body in the
relation between queerness, tactility, and touch.

Queer Touching

The idea that queer theory is a kind of touch has been formatively elaborated by
Carolyn Dinshaw in an essay titled "Chaucer's Queer Touches/A Queer Touches
Chaucer."[44] For Dinshaw, queerness can touch on bodies and cultural structures
alike, and its force on both is transformative. In this section I consider the critical
context of Dinshaw's argument, as well as its implications for the difficult relation
between queer theory and intersex bodies of diminished tactility. To be clear: I
am not referring here to a postsurgical diminution of sexuality or sex drive, even if
impaired tactility may sometimes correlate with such diminution.

   Writing on touch is often an occasion to comment on the human condition.
For instance, in a major book on the subject, the anthropologist Ashley Montagu
has advised gravely that "inadequate tactile experience will result in . . . inability
to relate to others in many fundamental human ways."[45] In this fashion touching
has frequently been presented as both figure and ground for interpersonal relations: it at once exemplifies relations and makes them possible. This is because
the touch, in Margrit Shildrick's words, is "an undecidable moment of exchange"
during which one's "sense of wholeness and self-sufficiency dissolve."[46] Here is
shattering not as asocial but conversely as the basis for sociality. Accordingly,
several feminists and queer theorists have celebrated the "conjoining power of
touch" as ethically and sexually superior to what Shildrick calls an "anaesthetic"
ethic grounded in "separation and division" that some critics have associated with
vision.[47] Conjoining is suggested by the syntax of Dinshaw's title "Chaucer's Queer
Touches/A Queer Touches Chaucer": it indicates that queer criticism will emerge
where author and critic touch. Undecidable exchange is stressed by Dinshaw's
substitution of an ambivalent slash for the conventional academic colon that would
hierarchize title and subtitle.

   The nonhierarchical configuration of text and critic indicates how touching connotes equality between individuals; similarly, Warner has used a spatial metaphor to claim that there is equality in shame, since in queer subcultures the indignity of sex is "spread around the room, leaving no one out, and in fact binding them together."[48] Shame here touches individuals and connects them, without separation and division, weblike. And just as there is no "sub" in Dinshaw's title, so too has Califia argued that queer sexual practices focused on touching are mutually respectful and nonhierarchical. During gay sex, writes Califia, "there's good sex, which includes lots of touching, and there's bad sex, which is nonsensual": touching is more than mere foreplay.[49] Consequently, in both the queer views on the relationship between bodies and pleasures that I discussed above, touching is crucial. While Blasius's model of sex that engages the entire body does demote the genitalia as the primary location of sexual activity, it simultaneously promotes touching just as much as the genital-centered behavior that it is intended to supersede.

Queer attention to touch is certainly an effective counterpoint to the medical project of making genitalia look normal at the cost of desensitization.[50] For example, in an anthology of writings on queer body image, Chase has eschewed the cultural use of "infant genitals . . . for discriminating male from female infants" on the grounds that "*my* genitals are for *my* pleasure."[51] In this respect queer theory lets us argue that desensitization is not an acceptable side effect of normalizing surgery, because genitalia are for touching, not for looking at. But implicit in this type of critique, whereby a medical concern for appearance is distinguished from a queer concern with touching, is a highly significant conflation of touch and tactility.[52] Touch and tactility are not the same: the former is an action, whereas the latter is a sense. Hence a body can touch without tactility, for instance, if one's hands are numb from exposure to cold weather. Likewise, a tactile body is not necessarily a body that is touched, as the figure of the stone butch exemplifies. Then again some bodies are indeed tactile, touching, and touched, all at once. My point is that touching and tactility are different, so they do not always coincide, although I recognize that for many bodies they do. Crucially, then, the conflation of touch and tactility is what enables a queer critique of surgery. This is because surgical desensitization impairs touching only if touching is assumed to entail tactility. After all, desensitized genitals can still touch and be touched; it is their tactility that surgery damages.

More than arguing for a queer critique of the impairment of tactility, I want to consider whether queerness itself is a kind of tactility or sensitivity to impressions. Elizabeth Freeman has recently called queer history "a structure of *tactile* feeling," and I am interested in whether postsurgical bodies can find a place within such a queer sensorial structure.[53] The shattering experience described by Bersani demonstrates that queer pleasure and shame are not necessarily opposed, for pleasure and shame are both "sensations of minority," to borrow a delightful phrase from Berlant.[54] As sensations, pleasure and shame have in common a position of exteriority to the social. In making this claim, my interest lies not in determining whether such sensations are inexorably antisocial but merely in suggesting that if pleasure and shame are embodied sensations, then by definition they are situated outside the social. They are in the body. For instance, critics have described shame as "an embodied emotion" that "makes our bodies horribly sensitive."[55] Meanwhile, Foucault has criticized the failure of "modern Western societies" to recognize "the reality of the body and the intensity of its pleasures."[56] All the same, the relation of exteriority that I'm describing is more complex than an opposition between body and society. I argue that queer sensations are exterior to the social as it has been defined in mainstream Western culture, because such sensations are cultivated through embodied participation in queer communities.[57]

Consider in this connection an account by Berlant and Warner of watching a performance of "erotic vomiting" at a leather bar. Describing the audience's transfixion, Berlant and Warner comment that "people are moaning softly with admiration, then whistling, stomping, screaming encouragements."[58] In other words, both the bodies of the performers and those of the audience are affected by the scene. For Berlant and Warner, this is the production, via sex in public, of "nonheteronormative bodily contexts" (208). The result is a queer community as the audience presses forward into "a compact and intimate group" of bodies before the performers (207). In light of this attention to the embodied sensations of minority, we can understand the Foucauldian emphasis on pleasure and the antisocial emphasis on shame (for surely both are in circulation during the erotic vomiting performance) as ways to privilege minority sensations. To be precise, such sensations not only signal but actually constitute a resistant relation to mainstream society. In other words, they have countercultural force.

Cultural change for Dinshaw is correspondingly accomplished not through touching alone but through the queer *sensation* of the touch. Berlant and Warner remark that heteronormativity can be unmarked, naturalized, and/or idealized (209n3), and it's Dinshaw's queer contestation of the second of these attributes — naturalization — that interests me most. She states that the "disillusioning force" of a queer character like Chaucer's Pardoner "shakes with his touch the heterocultural edifice": these sensory metaphors of shaking and force describe not only touching but moreover the tactile impression of being touched.[59] Similarly, Dinshaw asserts that twentieth-century readers of the Pardoner "can feel the shock" of the character's discourse and thereby "appropriate that power for queer use" (79). I suggest that queerness in Dinshaw's argument names the simultaneity of touching and tactility. Because of this simultaneity, queerness for Dinshaw can "provoke perceptual shifts and subsequent corporeal response in those touched" (76). It is through queer sensations, then, that cultural change is accomplished. As Dinshaw explains: "Queerness articulates not a determinate thing but a relation to existent structures of power. Despite its positioning on the other side of the law, it is arresting: it makes people stop and look at what they have been taking as natural" (77). It is as if bringing into relation "existent structures of power" and "the other side of the law" would enable some intermingling between these positions — as if making queerness and heteroculture touch could reveal the natural to be a construction after all. Now if one can relate to Shildrick's description of touching as an undecidable exchange in which self-sufficiency dissolves, then it's easy to imagine that when queerness and heteroculture touch, cultural change will happen. But with genitalia of diminished tactility, the catalytic (or shattering) potential of touching is far less clear. Dinshaw claims later that the queer touch renders strange "what has passed until now without comment" (79). I agree that queerness can have that disorienting effect, but what remains absolutely *not* strange in Dinshaw's queer analysis is the simultaneity of touching and tactility.

In summary, queerness as a critical kind of touching requires a tactile surface — whether of an individual subject or a cultural structure — for the registration of its contact. Evidently the conflation of touch and tactility may stigmatize as less than fully human (unable "to relate to others," as Montagu speculates) those individuals whose genitalia are without sensation. But that's not my main quarrel with this discourse. Rather, I would query the assumption that the body produced by normalizing genital surgery "passes without comment" and so is susceptible to queer denaturalization in the manner described by Dinshaw. If we think of surgery itself as touching, its effects are more ambivalent, so a different kind of critique will be necessary.

Queering Surgery

My critique of surgery in this section is intended to show why most queer accounts of touch are, in my view, insufficient for theorizing intersex. This is because not only recognizably queer touches defamiliarize. Indeed, touching may be defamiliarizing quite aside from its simultaneity with any particular sensation, as the surgical creation of insensate genitalia demonstrates. Put differently, the surgeon's desensitizing touch makes bodies strange.

To understand how genital surgery is a kind of touching, it's necessary first to analyze an implicit distinction in accounts such as Dinshaw's of the queer touch. The queer touch as discussed above is implicitly organized around a difference between cultural and natural, and therein lies a contradiction. On the one hand, the queer touch is cultural in its opposition to naturalized cultural structures: it transmits a denaturalizing constructivist force. But, on the other hand, the fact that the simultaneity of touching and tactility passes without comment in queer discourse is naturalizing: in this regard the queer touch seems beyond construction. This contradiction doesn't mean that we should give up trying to theorize queer touching, but it does suggest that we should shift the terms in which the touch is theorized away from the distinction between cultural and natural. This enables a more interesting critique of genital surgery, because such a critique will not depend on a judgment about whether surgery naturalizes or denaturalizes intersex genitalia.

With this purpose in mind I find extremely useful the "minoritizing" and "universalizing" terminology that Eve Kosofsky Sedgwick proposes in *Epistemology of the Closet*. The aim of her terminology is to address the question, "in whose lives is homo/heterosexual definition an issue of continuing centrality and difficulty?"[60] Or put another way: to whom is homosexuality important—homosexuals (in a minoritizing view) or everyone (in a universalizing view)? Whether one argues that the importance of homosexuality is natural or cultural is secondary. For example, everyone may be naturally homosexual, but most people may be socialized into heterosexuality; or only some people may be naturally homosexual, and the rest may be naturally heterosexual; or homosexuality may be an entirely cultural phenomenon; and so on. The value of Sedgwick's terminology is that it permits analysis of how and why the distinction between natural and cultural is used, rather than using that distinction as an explanatory framework. Sedgwick therefore offers these unusual terms as a wholesale alternative to "essentialist versus constructivist understandings of homosexuality" (40): whereas those understandings can lead to contradictions similar to the one I've identified in the queer touch, universalizing and minoritizing views of homosexuality can coexist without contradiction. Hence we can now see that Dinshaw universalizes the queer touch as "no one's property," shifting between characters and readers while simultaneously minoritizing it to twentieth-century critical readers who alone "can feel the shock" of a character such as the Pardoner.[61] The coexistence of universalization and minoritization in Dinshaw's account generates the denaturalizing power of the touch and also its naturalization: it is uniquely queer, yet it queers things for everybody. So the question I wish to ask is, to whom is touching important—queers or everyone?

Genital surgery for intersex is an example of how bodies touch. It is an embodied encounter between patients and surgeons.[62] The operating room, a space of stylized hygiene, makes possible extraordinarily intimate touches in which normally unseen and inaccessible bodily interiors are touched by other bodies and their technological prostheses.[63] Technology such as the scalpel extends the temporal reach of the surgeon's touch. The scalpel lends the surgeon's touch a force of which durability is an effect: by having the power to cut the body, the surgeon's touch persists in ways that would be impossible otherwise, changing for life the patient's genitalia.[64] In Ahmed's words, "the wound functions as a trace of where the surface of another entity . . . has impressed upon the body."[65] The corollary of this is the immobility of the patient's anesthetized body, which in its meaty docility is receptive to the impression of the touch. Giving willingly to the surgeon and medical team the ability to see oneself without being seen, during the time of anesthesia, is a corporeal gift that subverts the assumption by some critics that "the ability to see without being seen" is a "masculinist and imperialist" fascination.[66] Later, as the pain of wounds fades, the formation of scars constitutes a visual record of the cutting that anesthesia has hidden from the patient's memory.

In my opinion the touch of genital surgery on the body is strikingly similar to Esther Newton's account of how drag performers incongruously mix "sex-role referents" such as a tuxedo and earrings.[67] The performers in Newton's study called this "working with (feminine) pieces" (101), a phrase that I think describes what surgeons do when operating on intersex anatomies, although the "pieces" are not sartorial items but body parts, and not only feminine ones are manipulated. The surgeon's touch has the force to detach, move, reshape, and even injure such pieces. The resultant "drag" of surgery may take the form of contrasts between conventionally masculine and feminine genital parts, such as a phallus and labia, or it may take the form of juxtapositions between scarred tissue and undamaged flesh. Now it could be argued that genital surgery is a drag act that performatively produces gender by "dragging on" in the life of the postsurgical subject. In some instances this may be true. However, this is not my main point because I don't think we can assume that genital surgery necessarily has anything to do with gender. It may simply be stigmatizing, and that is all; gender may be formed by other means.[68]

Therefore this is drag not as disguise or impersonation but as a fragmentary working with pieces whereby the postsurgical body neither remains intersex nor becomes convincingly nonintersex. It is readable incongruously as both at once. The lived experience of this is that one's sexual anatomy seems both glaringly unusual and yet brutally normalized — one reason why postsurgical individuals may be fearful of sexual relations.[69] Surgery can leave one unsure as to whether an explanation for one's genital appearance and function needs to be offered to sexual partners—and if so, whether such an explanation should presume that partners have already noticed the effects of intersex, of surgery, or of both. The deficiency of the distinction between cultural and natural as a critical framework for understanding genital surgery also becomes apparent here: the postsurgical body is neither successfully constructed by surgery into a clearly male or female form, nor is it still naturally intersex. At the same time, depending on who is looking, the body's intersex condition may seem an unnatural residue that has not been adequately naturalized by surgery.[70] So the effect of the surgeon's touch is highly ambivalent in its production of persistently incongruous bodily "pieces"—masculine and feminine, intersexed and nonintersexed, presurgical and postsurgical.

For these reasons, one might even conclude that genital surgery makes bodies *more* intersex than they started out, as Holmes brilliantly puts it.[71] Certainly genital surgery can render strange anatomies that would otherwise have passed without comment. For instance, when I was about eleven, in the school locker-room (that fabled location on which some surgeons base judgments about the fate of intersexed people who don't receive surgery) I was teased *not* because of intersex characteristics that remained after surgery but specifically because of scars *caused* by surgery.[72] The copresence on my body's surface of presurgical and postsurgical times—the pieces of intersex alongside the pieces of surgery—made my intersex condition less notable but my body more strange. This was a nonheteronormative bodily context, in Berlant and Warner's phrase, if ever there was one. So although surgery is evidently an instrument of what Dinshaw calls heteroculture, I'd argue that it's nonetheless a queer practice according to her own definition. Surgery is an example of what Freeman has named "temporal drag"—the registration of "the co-presence of several historically-specific events" on bodily surfaces.[73]

The diminution of genital tactility is one way in which a historically specific event persists on the body's surface. As Ahmed explains in her book on the cultural politics of emotions, "It is through the recognition or interpretation of sensations, which are responses to the impressions of objects and others, that bodily surfaces take shape."[74] I think Ahmed is right, but she tells only half the story: I argue further that the body's very capacity for sensation is shaped by the impressions of objects and others on its surfaces. One such object is the surgeon's scalpel. It is not simply that we feel touches but that certain touches, depending on their force and durability, determine what we are able to feel. In this way I concur with Gayle Salamon that "as a perceived and perceiving entity, the body depends on a substratum of history."[75] Surgery's effects show how tactility, far from being simultaneous with touching, always has a constitutive history. A history of surgery forecloses the kinds of touches that a body can feel and drags the genitalia permanently back into the time of anesthetized insensitivity when surgery took place. Genital surgery thereby limits the extent to which the queer touch can be universalized to people with intersex bodies. Whether one regards surgery's aims and outcomes as naturalizing or denaturalizing, in matters of touch surgery is minoritizing, and I think this is reason enough to object to it.

The Time of the Reach

In this final section I consider what constraints desensitizing surgery places on the future for intersex bodies and show how queer theory might engage with desires that curiously persist after surgery. Halberstam has suggested that queer subcultures allow their participants "to believe that their futures can be imagined according to logics that lie outside of those paradigmatic markers of life experience — namely, birth, marriage, reproduction, and death."[76] There is an affinity here between queerness and intersex because both phenomena can disrupt the heterocultural scripts for birth, marriage, and reproduction. However, to accomplish this, queer subcultures tend to emphasize "flexibility" in desires, practices, and identifications, as Halberstam has noted elsewhere.[77] This leads to an opposition between flexibility and inflexibility, which in Halberstam's words "ascribes mobility over time to some notion of liberation and casts stubborn identification as a way of being stuck in time, unevolved, not versatile" (190). My concern as I draw to a close is not with identification (either as queer or as intersex) but with the flexible/inflexible binary itself. The queer touch is emblematic of flexibility because in Dinshaw's formulation it "moves around, is transferable," and can even work "across time."[78] I discuss whether the postsurgical body may be more flexible than a queer account might suggest, but I also argue that its flexibility shouldn't be the only measure of its future — or indeed the measure of only its future.

Even though the postsurgical body of diminished tactility is unquestionably material, it is still constructed, and in a queer reading this may imply a capacity for future change. As I've demonstrated, to say that the intersex body is constructed is to describe its materiality as contingent on the enduring touch of genital surgery. It's not to imply that the body is unreal but to tell the history of its realness — and thereby to insist that its realness is worth explaining. Contrary to most commentaries in the humanities on intersex, I offer this account not as a rejoinder to medicine but as a caution to queer theory. Queer theory as much as medicine has overlooked the construction of the tactile body (which includes the nurturing of tactility for some bodies as well as the destruction of tactility for others), despite the queer constructivist agenda and its attention to other aspects of the body's cultural formation. Moreover, there is no necessary relation between the revelation of the postsurgical body's construction and its deconstruction or reconstruction as something else. It may resist such constructive flexibility. So whereas queer theory often assumes that change follows from the revelation of construction, revealing the constructed character of the postsurgical intersex body makes possible no change: the insensate genitalia remain.[79]

In much queer theory, the idea of cultural change is sexualized as the hope for a future in which sex will take place, whether inside or outside the social. For example, Amber Hollibaugh has declared that "there is no human hope without the promise of ecstasy."[80] In this respect, I think Donald Morton was correct to state in his notorious 1995 *PMLA* essay on queer theory that "when queer theorists envision a future, they portray an ever-expanding region of sensuous pleasure, ignoring the historical constraints need places on pleasure."[81] Although I disagree with much of Morton's essay — in particular its simplification of the problems with queer politics to a flimsy opposition between "ludic" postmodernism and materialism (372) — I think he was right to critique the assumption that a queer future must be a "sensuous" one. But whereas Morton characterized the historical constraints on queer sensations as matters of material need, in the case of intersex a sensuous future is apparently closed down by the body's history of surgery. In other words, the problem with genital surgery for a queer account of intersex is surgery's foreclosure of the flexibility privileged in queer subcultures and exemplified by touching.

Nevertheless, to align what Salamon calls the body's "sedimented history" with material need versus ludic sensuality would be to give the postsurgical body an unwarranted inevitability.[82] My objection to this is not, for the reasons I explained in the previous section, that it would naturalize the body. Rather, I am concerned that a critique of queer sensations from the point of view of Morton's "historical materialism" would turn that critique into a reiteration of surgery's enduring effects.[83] Put another way, history would come to mean inflexibility. In Morton's attack on queer theory, history (as if this were a singular "systematic development," in his phrase [369]) becomes an explanation for pleasure's limits, and thereby imposes a limit of its own on critical analysis: history becomes the boundary beyond which critique cannot pass. Although Morton doesn't say so, this is because critique itself is a historical formation. So while history may explain why a sensuous future could be problematic, history's force as an explanation cannot be theorized in Morton's critical framework. Similarly, to represent the desensitized intersex body as the historical cause of a future without sex is to fail to imagine that anything other than tactility might organize sex. Therefore instead of critiquing queer theory in Morton's style by hammering it over the head with historical materialism, we might usefully unravel the opposition between historical inflexibility and queer flexibility.

Desire unravels this opposition, I believe. Consider that a diminution or loss of genital sensation may have nothing to do with desire, which might function independently of tactility. David Reimer, whose alleged sex reassignment from male to female after a circumcision accident was often cited as proof of surgery's capacity to change gender identity in children with unusual genitalia, has described the persistence of desire following the removal of his penis.[84] "If you lose your arm," he explained to his biographer, "and you're dying of thirst, that stump is still going to move toward that glass of water to try to get it. It's instinct. It's in you."[85] In this comment Reimer differentiates between desire and history, but for Reimer, unlike Morton, these are not mutually exclusive. Morton regards desire in queer and postmodern theory as "an autonomous entity outside history," opposed to historically determined need.[86] Desire in Reimer's account, though, is neither wholly inside nor wholly outside history, for it is the experience of the past's failure to determine fully the present. Therefore although history persists in the present by leaving the postsurgical individual with a "stump" (whether literally or metaphorically), the stump may be invested with desire in ways that could not be anticipated by a historical materialist explanation of how the stump came to be. Put another way, desire arises from the difference between past and present, but it cannot be reduced to an effect of the past on the present. Desire in my analysis is therefore separate from the question of how we might imagine and reach a queer future.[87] It is a matter of how we reach and inhabit the present.

So desire is also distinct from the issue of how we might pursue and archive a queer history as Dinshaw envisages it.[88] At first glance, Reimer's account is akin to Dinshaw's theory of the queer touch: a text such as the *Canterbury Tales* may activate and engage readerly desires that cannot be explained by history of the text. These desires arise when text and critic come into contact across time, as Dinshaw states. Yet there is a key difference between Dinshaw and Reimer: the former describes touching; the latter, reaching. Although the reach doesn't "move around" quite like the touch, it is nevertheless a dynamic "moving toward," to use Reimer's phrase. Desire in this way cannot be reduced to an embodied affect, for its situation is neither in the postsurgical body nor in the presurgical body. Instead, desire names a relation between these bodies for the individual who inhabits the narrative of their succession. Reimer's narrative of reaching interest-

ingly demonstrates both the flexibility of desire and also desire's stubbornness—
its persistence after genital modification signals its adaptability just as much as
its intractability. This account of desire thereby confounds the canonical queer
binary between flexibility and immobility.

Edelman has argued that queer theory should "remind us that we are
inhabited always by states of desire that exceed our capacity to name them."[89] If
Edelman is correct, then I think a queer understanding of the postsurgical body
need *not* attend to the genitalia on which surgery operates, and which surgery
attempts to name as female or male for heterosexist ends. Other types of critique,
such as those from feminist science studies, can make those complaints.[90] A queer
understanding ought to attend instead to the desires that exceed such naming.
Otherwise, queer theory may echo the medical attempt to normalize bodies as
markers of dichotomously sexed heterosexual desire by attempting to locate in
bodies the nonheteronormative sensations of minority. What queer theory can do
for intersex, then, is critique genital surgery without presuming to know in advance
what comes after surgery, after desensitization, or even after queer theory—shame
or pleasure; naturalization or denaturalization; familiarization or defamiliar-
ization.[91] Queerness is useful instead for its interrogation of the meaning of the
"after," which is the flexibility and inflexibility of history in the present.

Notes

I thank Neil Badmington, Jake Buckley, Sarah Creighton, Rebecca Munford, and
Margrit Shildrick for helpful information and discussions, and the *GLQ* anonymous
reviewers for perceptive feedback.

1. Sarah E. Chinn, "Feeling Her Way: Audre Lorde and the Power of Touch," *GLQ* 9
    (2003): 192.
2. Cheryl Chase, letter to the editor, *Journal of Urology* 156 (1996): 1139; see also Mor-
    gan Holmes, "Rethinking the Meaning and Management of Intersexuality," *Sexuali-
    ties* 5 (2002): 163.
3. N. S. Crouch et al., "Genital Sensation after Feminizing Genitoplasty for Congenital
    Adrenal Hyperplasia: A Pilot Study," *British Journal of Urology International* 93
    (2004): 137.
4. J. P. Gearhart, A. Burnett, and J. H. Owen, letter to the editor, *Journal of Urology* 156
    (1996): 1140.
5. Alain Borgeat, Georgios Ekatodramis, and Carlo A. Schenker, "Postoperative Nau-
    sea and Vomiting in Regional Anesthesia: A Review," *Anesthesiology* 98 (2003):
    530–47.

6. Gillian Einstein, "From Body to Brain: Considering the Neurobiological Effects of Female Genital Cutting," *Perspectives in Biology and Medicine* 51 (2008): 84–97.

7. Rakesh Kapoor et al., "Sigmoid Vaginoplasty: Long-Term Results," *Journal of Urology* 67 (2006): 1212–15.

8. Robert Jensen, "Getting It Up for Politics: Gay Male Sexuality and Radical Lesbian Feminism," in *Opposite Sex: Gay Men on Lesbians, Lesbians on Gay Men*, ed. Sara Miles and Eric Rofes (New York: New York University Press, 1998), 165.

9. Sara Ahmed, *Strange Encounters: Embodied Others in Post-Coloniality* (New York: Routledge, 2000), 155.

10. David M. Halperin, *What Do Gay Men Want? An Essay on Sex, Risk, and Subjectivity* (Ann Arbor: University of Michigan Press, 2007), 86.

11. Michael Warner, *The Trouble with Normal: Sex, Politics, and the Ethics of Queer Life* (Cambridge, MA: Harvard University Press, 1999), 37.

12. Lee Edelman, "Queer Theory: Unstating Desire," *GLQ* 2 (1995): 345.

13. Pat Califia, "A Secret Side of Lesbian Sexuality," in *Public Sex: The Culture of Radical Sex*, 2nd ed. (San Francisco: Cleis, 2000), 166.

14. Intersex Society of North America, "Why Doesn't ISNA Want to Eradicate Gender?" (2006), www.isna.org/faq/not_eradicating_gender. My claim here is not that queer theory has had nothing to say about gender but that it has critiqued gender for the perceived limitations that it places on sex and sexuality. Accordingly, and unlike much second-wave feminism, queer theory has generally argued that gender identities should be "fucked" (blended, dissolved, crossed, and so on) instead of more equitably defined. See, for example, Stephen Whittle, "Gender Fucking or Fucking Gender?" in *Queer Theory*, ed. Iain Morland and Annabelle Willox (Basingstoke: Palgrave, 2005), 115–29.

15. Donald Morton, "Birth of the Cyberqueer," *PMLA* 110 (1995): 370. Although I think Morton is right on this point, I have reservations about much of his essay, which I discuss below.

16. See, for example, Betsy Driver, preface to special issue, *Cardozo Journal of Law and Gender* 12 (2005): 3; Peter Hegarty in conversation with Cheryl Chase, "Intersex Activism, Feminism, and Psychology: Opening a Dialogue on Theory, Research, and Clinical Practice," *Feminism & Psychology* 10 (2000): 127; Morgan Holmes, "Queer Cut Bodies," in *Queer Frontiers: Millennial Geographies, Genders, and Generations*, ed. Joseph A. Boone et al. (Madison: University of Wisconsin Press, 2000), 98; Emi Koyama, *Intersex Critiques: Notes on Intersex, Disability, and Biomedical Ethics* (Portland: Confluere, 2003), 3, 7, 15.

17. John P. Gearhart, quoted in M. M. Bailez et al., "Vaginal Reconstruction after Initial Construction of the External Genitalia in Girls with Salt-Wasting Adrenal Hyperplasia," *Journal of Urology* 148 (1992): 684; W. Hardy Hendren and Anthony Atala, "Repair of High Vagina in Girls with Severely Masculinized Anatomy from the Adrenogenital Syndrome," *Journal of Pediatric Surgery* 30 (1995): 91.

18. M. Morgan Holmes, "Queer Cut Bodies: Intersexuality and Homophobia in Medical Practice" (1995), tinyurl.com/6aw334. Note that this version differs from Holmes's chapter of the same name in *Queer Frontiers*.

19. Douglas Crimp, "Melancholia and Moralism," in *Loss: The Politics of Mourning*, ed. David L. Eng and David Kazanjian (Berkeley: University of California Press, 2002), 199.

20. The most influential articulation of "resignification" as a third-wave feminist/queer practice is in Judith Butler's *Gender Trouble: Feminism and the Subversion of Identity*, 2nd ed. (New York: Routledge, 1999), 42.

21. Pat Califia, "Genderbending: Playing with Roles and Reversals," in *Public Sex: The Culture of Radical Sex*, 2nd ed. (San Francisco: Cleis, 2000), 185.

22. David M. Halperin, *Saint Foucault: Towards a Gay Hagiography* (New York: Oxford University Press, 1995), 26. I find Halperin's account informative, but it also has limitations, which are demonstrated by Halperin's suggestion that "Foucault's focus on sexuality, and his refusal to subordinate the analysis of its instrumentality to the politics of gender, race, or class, made his work particularly useful for addressing the irreducibly *sexual* politics of the AIDS crisis" (27). While this focus on the sexual may seem paradigmatically queer (and as Halperin clarifies in a note, it enables an analysis of homophobia [195n26]), it for the same reason fails to consider how the other kinds of politics mentioned by Halperin not only affect sexuality but constitute the sexual *as* irreducible for particular subjects. In fact in his later book *What Do Gay Men Want?* Halperin acknowledges that "the focus on gay subjectivity [in public discourse on HIV/AIDS prevention] is sharpest in the case of white, socially privileged gay men, whose agency and autonomy are not likely to have been compromised by political oppression or external constraint and whose behavior therefore cannot be explained by other social factors" (23). But even this later formulation is somewhat unsatisfactory; I would suggest that uncompromised agency and autonomy are indeed explicable by "other social factors" such as race, class, and gender (see, for example, Damien W. Riggs, *Priscilla, (White) Queen of the Desert: Queer Rights/Race Privilege* [New York: Peter Lang, 2006]). Judith Halberstam offers a provocative analysis of such ongoing tensions in queer identity politics in "Shame and Gay White Masculinity," *Social Text* 23, nos. 3–4 (2005): 219–33.

23. Michel Foucault, *The Will to Knowledge*, vol. 1 of *The History of Sexuality*, trans. Robert Hurley (Harmondsworth, UK: Penguin, 1998), 155, 157.

24. Lauren Berlant, *The Queen of America Goes to Washington City: Essays on Sex and Citizenship* (Durham, NC: Duke University Press, 1997), 158.

25. Tim Dean, *Beyond Sexuality* (Chicago: University of Chicago Press, 2000), 172.

26. Mark Blasius, *Gay and Lesbian Politics: Sexuality and the Emergence of a New Ethic* (Philadelphia: Temple University Press, 1994), 110. See also pages 125 and 221 on the "queerness" of Blasius's "new ethic."

27. Blasius, *Gay and Lesbian Politics*, 125; see also Michael Bronski, *The Pleasure Principle: Sex, Backlash, and the Struggle for Gay Freedom* (New York: St. Martin's, 1998), 157. On the Foucauldian basis of this claim, see Michel Foucault, "Sex, Power, and the Politics of Identity," interview by B. Gallagher and A. Wilson, in *Ethics: Subjectivity and Truth*, vol. 1 of *The Essential Works of Foucault, 1954–1984*, ed. Paul Rabinow, trans. Robert Hurley et al. (New York: New Press, 1997), 163–73, esp. 164–65.

28. Amber Hollibaugh, in Deirdre English, Amber Hollibaugh, and Gayle Rubin, "Talking Sex: A Conversation on Sexuality and Feminism," *Feminist Review* 11 (June 1982): 44.

29. Cheryl Chase, "Affronting Reason," in *Looking Queer*, ed. Dawn Atkins (New York: Harrington Park, 1998), 207.

30. Beyond the context of intersex, Jensen has made a comparable criticism of gay male culture ("Getting It Up for Politics," 166).

31. Sally R. Munt, "Shame/Pride Dichotomies in *Queer as Folk*," *Textual Practice* 14 (2000): 533, 536.

32. Leo Bersani, "Is the Rectum a Grave?" in *AIDS: Cultural Analysis/Cultural Activism*, ed. Douglas Crimp (Cambridge, MA: MIT Press, 1988), 197–98.

33. Bersani, "Is the Rectum a Grave?" 222; Kathryn Bond Stockton, *Beautiful Bottom, Beautiful Shame: Where "Black" Meets "Queer"* (Durham, NC: Duke University Press, 2006), 15.

34. Bersani, "Is the Rectum a Grave?" 212; see also Stockton, *Beautiful Bottom*, 15.

35. Robert L. Caserio, "The Antisocial Thesis in Queer Theory," *PMLA* 121 (2006): 819–21.

36. Leo Bersani, *Homos* (Cambridge, MA: Harvard University Press, 1995), 93; see also 94.

37. Stockton, *Beautiful Bottom*, 15. The antisocial relationship between negativity and futurity has been most polemically explored by Lee Edelman in *No Future: Queer Theory and the Death Drive* (Durham, NC: Duke University Press, 2004).

38. Warner, *Trouble with Normal*, 35, 36.

39. Bersani, *Homos*, 80; Stockton, *Beautiful Bottom*, 15.

40. Heather Love, *Feeling Backward: Loss and the Politics of Queer History* (Cambridge, MA: Harvard University Press, 2007), 40. However, Love does ultimately seem to recuperate as "bound up with pleasure" the emotions associated with an aversion to sex (161).

41. Judith Halberstam, "Lesbian Masculinity, or Even Stone Butches Get the Blues," *Women and Performance* 8, no. 2 (1996): 64.

42. Halberstam, "Lesbian Masculinity," 68; Ann Cvetkovich, *An Archive of Feelings: Trauma, Sexuality, and Lesbian Public Cultures* (Durham, NC: Duke University Press, 2003), 67.

43. Ellen K. Feder, "Imperatives of Normality: From 'Intersex' to 'Disorders of Sex Development,'" this issue. Some people do identify as "intersex" or "intersexual," of course, and I used both terms throughout "Is Intersexuality Real?" (*Textual Practice* 15 [2001]: 527–47). But I still don't think either term is comparable to *homosexual* because a sexual identity is just one of many things to which the terms could refer—anatomies (pre- and postsurgical), desires, gender identifications and roles, and so on. In particular to say that "intersex" names a sexual identity specific to a certain anatomy is to insinuate that all sexual identities are based in anatomy.

44. Carolyn Dinshaw, "Chaucer's Queer Touches/A Queer Touches Chaucer," *Exemplaria* 7 (1995): 75–92.

45. Ashley Montagu, *Touching: The Human Significance of the Skin* (New York: Columbia University Press, 1971), 292.

46. Margrit Shildrick, "Unreformed Bodies: Normative Anxiety and the Denial of Pleasure," *Women's Studies* 34 (2005): 329.

47. Chinn, "Feeling Her Way," 195; Margrit Shildrick, *Embodying the Monster: Encounters with the Vulnerable Self* (London: Sage, 2002), 119; Iris Marion Young, "The Scaling of Bodies and the Politics of Identity," in *Space, Gender, Knowledge: Feminist Readings*, ed. Linda McDowell and Joanne P. Sharp (London: Arnold, 1997), 221.

48. Warner, *Trouble with Normal*, 36.

49. Pat Califia, "Gay Men, Lesbians, and Sex: Doing It Together," in *Public Sex: The Culture of Radical Sex*, 2nd ed. (San Francisco: Cleis, 2000), 194.

50. For a further analysis of the extent to which surgery creates "normal-looking" genitalia, see Iain Morland, "The Injustice of Intersex: Feminist Science Studies and the Writing of a Wrong," in *Toward a Critique of Guilt: Perspectives from Law and the Humanities*, ed. Matthew Anderson (New York: Elsevier, 2005), 60–62.

51. Chase, "Affronting Reason," 210.

52. In this discussion I use the term *tactility* rather than *feeling* to avoid additional conflation with affect. Other critics have argued for the interrelation of tactility and affect. Eve Sedgwick in a book called *Touching Feeling* has suggested that the verbs in her book's title carry a double meaning, "tactile plus emotional." To be sure, the words may bear double meanings, but it doesn't follow that the tactile and affective realms are necessarily interconnected. Nonetheless, Sedgwick continues that "a particular intimacy seems to subsist between textures and emotions." Even though she advances this claim as "intuition" rather than a fact, it's unsatisfactorily circular because it attempts to explain touching (as tactile, textural) in terms of touching (as the affective intuition of a proximate "intimacy"). See Eve Kosofsky Sedgwick, *Touching Feeling: Affect, Pedagogy, Performativity* (Durham, NC: Duke University Press, 2003), 17. For a further argument about the significance of affect to queer theory and sexualities, see Ann Cvetkovich, "Public Feelings," *South Atlantic Quarterly* 106 (2007): 459–68.

53. Elizabeth Freeman, "Time Binds, or, Erotohistoriography," *Social Text* 23, nos. 3–4 (2005): 66; emphasis in original.

54. Lauren Berlant, "68 or The Revolution of Little Queers," in *Feminism Beside Itself*, ed. Diane Elam and Robyn Wiegman (New York: Routledge, 1995), 301.

55. Noreen Giffney, preface (with Michael O'Rourke) to Sally R. Munt, *Queer Attachments: The Cultural Politics of Shame* (Aldershot, UK: Ashgate, 2008), ix; Elspeth Probyn, *Blush: Faces of Shame* (Minneapolis: University of Minnesota Press, 2005), 127.

56. Michel Foucault, introduction to *Herculine Barbin: Being the Recently Discovered Memoirs of a Nineteenth-Century French Hermaphrodite*, trans. Richard McDougall (New York: Pantheon, 1980), vii.

57. Of course, sensations of pleasure and shame can equally be firmly mainstream—for example, the visceral titillation, for some, of watching a heteronormative movie.

58. Lauren Berlant and Michael Warner, "Sex in Public," in *Publics and Counterpublics*, by Michael Warner (New York: Zone, 2002), 207.

59. Dinshaw, "Chaucer's Queer Touches," 92, 89.

60. Eve Kosofsky Sedgwick, *Epistemology of the Closet* (Berkeley: University of California Press, 1990), 40.

61. Dinshaw, "Chaucer's Queer Touches," 79.

62. Rosalyn Diprose, *Corporeal Generosity: On Giving with Nietzsche, Merleau-Ponty, and Levinas* (New York: State University of New York Press, 2002), 107–21.

63. For a seminal account of the stylized aspects of the operating room, see Pearl Katz, "Ritual in the Operating Room," *Ethnology* 20 (1981): 335–50.

64. Another way to theorize this durability is as a kind of writing. See Iain Morland, "'The Glans Opens Like a Book': Writing and Reading the Intersexed Body," *Continuum* 19 (2005): 335–48.

65. Sara Ahmed, *The Cultural Politics of Emotion* (Edinburgh: Edinburgh University Press, 2004), 27.

66. Chinn, "Feeling Her Way," 195.

67. Esther Newton, *Mother Camp: Female Impersonators in America* (Chicago: University of Chicago Press, 1979), 101.

68. Alice Domurat Dreger, *Hermaphrodites and the Medical Invention of Sex* (Cambridge, MA: Harvard University Press, 1998), 200.

69. See, for example, Mary E. Boyle, Susan Smith, and Lih-Mei Liao, "Adult Genital Surgery for Intersex: A Solution to What Problem?" *Journal of Health Psychology* 10 (2005): 573–84; and Lih-Mei Liao, "Learning to Assist Women Born with Atypical Genitalia: Journey through Ignorance, Taboo, and Dilemma," *Journal of Reproductive and Infant Psychology* 21 (2003): 233.

70. For another account of how intersex is "constructed," see Morland, "Is Intersexuality Real?" 533.

71. Holmes, "Rethinking the Meaning," 174; on the failure of surgery to "normalize," see also Holmes, "Queer Cut Bodies" (*Queer Frontiers* version), 104.

72. On the rhetoric of the "locker-room" in medical discourse about intersex, see Iain Morland, "Plastic Man: Intersex, Humanism, and the Reimer Case," *Subject Matters* 3–4 (2007): 82–83.

73. Elizabeth Freeman, "Packing History, Count(er)ing Generations," *New Literary History* 31 (2000): 728, 729; see also Freeman's ingenious analysis of Frankenstein's monster's body as the literalization of the queer touch ("Time Binds," 60). I'd prefer not to argue that postsurgical bodies are Frankensteinian. In future work I'll discuss in more detail the bodily coexistence of different time periods after surgery, including the relation between body parts with and without tactility.

74. Ahmed, *Cultural Politics*, 25.

75. Gayle Salamon, "Boys of the Lex: Transgenderism and Rhetorics of Materiality," *GLQ* 12 (2006): 583.

76. Judith Halberstam, *In a Queer Time and Place: Transgender Bodies, Subcultural Lives* (New York: New York University Press, 2005), 2.

77. Judith Halberstam, "Theorizing Queer Temporalities: A Roundtable Discussion," Carolyn Dinshaw et al., *GLQ* 13 (2007): 190.

78. Dinshaw, "Chaucer's Queer Touches," 79; Carolyn Dinshaw, *Getting Medieval: Sexualities and Communities, Pre- and Postmodern* (Durham, NC: Duke University Press, 1999), 21.

79. As Love argues, "Critics [in queer studies] have ignored what they could not transform" (*Feeling Backward*, 147).

80. Amber Hollibaugh, "My Dangerous Desires: Falling in Love with Stone Butches, Passing Women, and Girls (Who Are Guys) Who Catch My Eye," in *Queer Cultures*, ed. Deborah Carlin and Jennifer DiGrazia (Upper Saddle River, NJ: Pearson Prentice Hall, 2004), 383.

81. Morton, "Birth of the Cyberqueer," 375.

82. Salamon, "Boys of the Lex," 583.

83. Morton, "Birth of the Cyberqueer," 369.

84. For a full account of the Reimer case in relation to intersex treatment, see Morland, "Plastic Man."

85. John Colapinto, *As Nature Made Him: The Boy Who Was Raised as a Girl* (London: Quartet, 2000), 148.

86. Morton, "Birth of the Cyberqueer," 371.

87. Kate Thomas has described the movement to a queer future as a sensation of reaching—a "muscular, epistemic stretch" ("Post Sex: On Being Too Slow, Too Stupid, Too Soon," *South Atlantic Quarterly* 106 [2007]: 623–24).

88. Desire in my account is also slightly different to the psychoanalytic argument about historical practice and the past made by Valerie Traub in *The Renaissance of Lesbi-*

anism in Early Modern England (Cambridge: Cambridge University Press, 2002), 353–54.

89. Edelman, "Queer Theory," 345.

90. See Morland, "Injustice of Intersex."

91. A recent special issue of *South Atlantic Quarterly*, titled "After Queer Theory," engages with some of these questions of queerness, although intersex is mentioned only once, and in passing, in the issue (Carla Freccero, "Queer Times," *South Atlantic Quarterly* 106 [2007]: 491).

THE SOMATECHNICS OF INTERSEXUALITY

Nikki Sullivan

Intersex in the Age of Ethics
Alice Domurat Dreger, ed.
Hagerstown, MD: University Publishing Group, 1999. x + 227 pp.

Surgically Shaping Children: Technology, Ethics, and the Pursuit of Normality
Erik Parens, ed.
Baltimore: Johns Hopkins University Press, 2006. xxx + 274 pp.

Ethics and Intersex
Sharon E. Sytsma, ed.
Dordrecht: Springer, 2006. xxv + 336 pp.

*W*e live in a world in which, as John Jordan has noted, "the body" is conceived as plastic, a malleable substance in a state of potential transition.[1] We are surrounded by, and have embodied, the idea that while the vast majority of bodies may not be ill, they are nevertheless "wrong" in one way or another: they have too few (or too many) limbs or digits; they (or parts of them) are the wrong size, the wrong age, the wrong color; they are "sexually ambiguous"; they bear the wrong ethnic markers; they inhibit particular identities and/or aspirations; they simply do not seem "right." Surgery, then, becomes a means of correcting things, of restoring order. But the plastic body, as Kevin Michael De Luca has argued, is the site and substance of contestation, of argument itself, and nowhere is this clearer than in recent debates about genital modification—in particular, surgeries performed on infants too young to consent.[2]

GLQ 15:2
DOI 10.1215/10642684-2008-140
© 2009 by Duke University Press

While the writing to date on modificatory surgeries is immensely varied, the vast majority is subtended by a conception of medical practices and procedures as technologies separate from the bodies they seek to modify. In this model, the body is a fleshly substrate that simply *is* prior to its enhancement or mutilation by the technologies that transform its original state. Even in much scholarship that recognizes a heterogeneity of effects produced by technological intervention, there nevertheless remains the often implicit assumption that bodies and technologies are fundamentally separate entities. However, there are those who argue, as Anna Munster has, that technologies are "always in a dynamic relation to the matter which gives [them their] substance and to the other machines—aesthetic, social, economic—which substantiate [them] as . . . ensemble[s]."[3] Further, insofar as technologies are always already inextricably bound up with systems of power/ knowledge, they do not stand outside the subject but are constitutive of the very categories integral to constructing subjectivities, categories "such as the real, the natural and the body" (122). In short, what has begun to emerge in and through critiques of popular commonsense understandings of the body, technology, and the relation between them is the notion of a chiasmic interdependence of soma and techné: of bodily-being (or corporealities) as always already technologized and technologies as always already enfleshed. And here technologies are never simply "machinic" as they so often appear to be in the popular imagination. Rather, technés are necessarily epistemic: as Lily Kay puts it, "technology and theory generate each other, epistemic things become technical things and vice versa."[4]

This article deploys the term *somatechnics* to think through the varied and complex ways in which bodily-being is shaped not only by the surgeon's knife but also by the discourses that justify and contest the use of such instruments. In arguing that the conceptions of, debates around, and questions about specific modificatory practices are themselves technologies that shape corporeality at the most profound level, I aim to make a critical intervention into, and open up new spaces for reflection in, existing debates about the somatechnics of intersexuality. In doing so, I recognize that my contribution is no less an effect of the operations of power particular to a given time and place—the somatechnologies, if you like—than the work with which I engage. In other words, I acknowledge that the critical practice I perform itself contributes to the formation and transformation of bodies (of flesh, knowledge, politic) in heterogenerative and unpredictable ways. As such, the intervention I make should not be understood in terms of a definitive answer to a set of identifiable universalizable problems but as a necessarily delimited offering that is open to ongoing (re)evaluation and modification. I approach the collections under review with this double understanding of somatechnics as

systematized operations of power/knowledge/practice and as an open-ended critical methodology necessarily implicated in the former.

It has been a decade since the publication of Alice Domurat Dreger's
landmark edited collection, *Intersex in the Age of Ethics*—a collection in which,
for the first time, the voices of intersex people figure centrally in the genealogi-
cal investigations of the ways in which intersexuality has come to matter. At the
time of publication the collection, which critiques from a range of perspectives
the "techno-centric treatment paradigm," performed what Foucault refers to
as the "insurrection of subjugated knowledges."[5] Foucault uses this term in two
distinct yet connected ways, to refer both to those "local" knowledges that have
been disqualified as subjective, naive, and/or "below the required level of scien-
tificity" and also to "blocks of historical knowledge"—that is, technés—that are
"present in functional and systematic ensembles" but are masked (7). In giving
voice to those whose corporeality has literally been carved out via the technologies of medicine, and in bringing to light the knowledges that shape such operations, this collection continues to play an integral role in desubjugation, enabling
subjugated knowledges "to oppose and struggle against the coercion of a unitary,
formal, and scientific theoretical discourse" (9).

In *Hermaphrodites and the Medical Invention of Sex*, a monograph published twelve months before *Intersex in the Age of Ethics*, Dreger had suggested that
such "insurrection" is coextensive with related developments particular to "postmodern times."[6] These include the (re)valuation of voices and knowledges previously disqualified, the recognition of meaning as necessarily heterogeneous (as
opposed to the notion of truth as singular), the reconception of medicine (like other
institutions) as a functional and systematic ensemble in and through which power
operates, a shift in the conception of "the doctor," "the patient," and the relations
between them, and an increasing acceptance of constructivist insights.[7] But despite
the shifts mapped and enabled by these texts and the ongoing political struggles of
those individuals and organizations who contributed to their emergence, the kinds
of medical and epistemological reforms envisaged by Dreger and others a decade
ago have not occurred to the extent they had hoped. As Dreger herself notes in an
essay published in Sharon E. Sytsma's collection *Ethics and Intersex*, "changing
the treatment of intersex has turned out to be a much harder job than those of us in
the early intersex reform movement imagined it would be."[8] Indeed, this difficulty
in shifting firmly entrenched attitudes and practices (both medical and social) is
evidenced by the very existence of *Ethics and Intersex*, a collection whose raison
d'être echoes that of *Intersex in the Age of Ethics*.

Ethics and Intersex aims, writes Sytsma, "to provide a multi-disciplinarian and multi-cultural approach to intersexuality," and to this end it includes contributions from psychiatrists, biologists, philosophers, theologians, legal scholars, endocrinologists, gynecologists, bioethicists, pediatricians, and critical theorists.[9] The result is a collection whose diversity is, for me at least, at once laudable and yet strangely troubling: troubling perhaps because while its stated goal is "to improve the quality of life for intersexual people," it does not constitute—at least not in the way or to the extent that *Intersex in the Age of Ethics* could be said to—a call to arms by voices unified (although not univalent) in the challenges they pose to medicalization. One could argue that this is less a problem endemic to the text than a problem of perception or expectation, since, as Iain Morland suggests in "Postmodern Intersex," "the ethical tenor of [the] reformist project comes not from its advocacy of a categorical imperative that abolishes ambivalence, but from the project's own enactment of the fact that in postmodern times, even the most categorical of imperatives is inescapably ambivalent."[10] As I argue in due course, however, while *Ethics and Intersex* as a collection is diverse, it does not effectively or explicitly mobilize the fact of its heterogeneity in terms of a postmodern or postconventional ethics.[11]

Like *Ethics and Intersex* as a whole, Dreger's contribution, "Intersex and Human Rights: The Long View," is concerned with opening out the question of intersexuality to maximize the potential for reform. But while the focus of *Ethics and Intersex* (as a collection) repeats the common tendency to partition intersexuality and the somatechnologies that constitute it from other bodies and somatic practices, Dreger's article attempts to undo such a move. Frustrated by the fact that reform has not occurred as rapidly or to the extent hoped for, Dreger reconsiders some of the assumptions that informed her earlier work, in particular the outraged claim made in a 1998 publication that "the treatment of intersex [is] unlike anything else in modern-day medicine."[12] While a decade later Dreger is no less appalled by what she sees as the continued inhumane (medical) (mis) treatment of intersex infants, she is now of the opinion that in fact "the treatment of intersex actually looks a lot like other realms of modern medicine" (75). She argues that the withholding of information, for example, occurs in a range of medical settings—in particular, pediatric care. And perhaps more disturbing still is the existence of "normalizing" surgeries routinely performed on otherwise healthy children, surgeries that in many cases parents and medical practitioners genuinely believe are both necessary and beneficial. Indeed, this congruence—the fact that, rather than being an isolated and aberrant instance, the treatment of intersex is in keeping with other somatechnologies—may well explain why a moratorium on the medically unnecessary modification of the bodies (and lives) of intersex children too young to participate in decision-making processes has not yet taken place.

How then might we respond to the insight that the somatechnologies of intersexuality—the operations of both micro and macro power that constitute intersex embodiment and its treatment in historically and culturally specific ways—are neither distinct from nor categorically different from a range of other modificatory procedures, the knowledges that inform them, and the bodies (both individual and social) they engender? The answer is numerously. One response might involve juxtaposing various modificatory procedures, the justifications that inform their practice or its prohibition and the ethico-political lived effects of such, in the hope that in so doing, questions, issues, and insights associated with one particular practice may cast new light on others. This may in turn engender more-nuanced understandings of and critical responses to the complex and multi-faceted technés in and through which embodied being(s) comes to matter in situated contextually specific ways. This is what Erik Parens's collection, *Surgically Shaping Children: Technology, Ethics, and the Pursuit of Normality*, sets out to do and what in my opinion it successfully achieves.

Surgically Shaping Children comes out of a project undertaken by the Hastings Center designed to explore critically the ethical questions surrounding the use of surgery to normalize children whose bodies are conceived as anomalous (rather than simply atypical). More specifically, the collection focuses on three conditions generally perceived as "disabling"—intersexuality, achondroplasia (or dwarfism), and cleft lips and palates—and on the "tension between the obligations to let children be and to shape them."[13] As Parens recounts it, this bringing together of the particular forms of surgical shaping associated with the aforementioned "conditions," of procedures both controversial and relatively uncontested, "turn[ed] out to complicate—and thereby deepen" the reflections of those involved in the project (xiv). The project of which *Surgically Shaping Children* is a product was also shaped by two other Hastings Center studies, one on the ethics of prenatal testing and the other on the "enhancement" of human traits. While the somatechnologies explored in these earlier studies are not discussed explicitly in *Surgically Shaping Children*, the critical analyses in Parens's volume do provide a backdrop against which the focus of this particular collection emerges. Consequently, the collection as a whole provides a complex picture of how notions of conformity and individualism, shame and pride, enhancement and mutilation, health and sickness, are mobilized in a variety of complex and often contradictory ways. At the same time it shows that particular conceptions of individual rights, parental responsibility, medical ethics, moral law, choice, self-fulfillment, and authenticity are specific to the here and now, to the epistemological "truths" that shape our embodiment no less than the knife of the surgeon.

Like *Intersex in the Age of Ethics* Parens's collection is informed by an ethico-political commitment to foreground the voices of those most intimately affected by the modificatory procedures in question. But in *Surgically Shaping Children* this commitment extends to address in detail the experience of parenting atypically embodied children. For example, whereas Dreger's collection includes some relevant but brisk bullet-pointed advice to clinicians from one parent of an intersex child, and an interview conducted with an intersex woman and her mother, *Surgically Shaping Children* features three substantial first-person narratives by parents — one of whom, Cassandra Aspinall, is herself affected by the "condition" she shares with a son.[14] This inclusion is crucial not least because it enables an articulation of the embodiedness of situated knowledges, which in turn helps explain why simply exposing what one might see as "the immoral status of the dominant medical model" has not resulted in the immediate wholesale abandonment of infant surgical sex assignment.[15]

While the relation between parenting, medical technology, and embodiment is explored throughout Parens's collection, it is approached in a particularly thought-provoking way in Ellen K. Feder's contribution, " 'In Their Best Interests': Parents' Experience of Atypical Genitalia," in which the author explains the success of "the imperative of normality" via an explication of Pierre Bourdieu's account of habitus.[16] Feder begins by recounting two studies conducted by Suzanne Kessler: in the first, female college students were asked to imagine that they had been born with an unusually large clitoris, and male students to imagine that they had been born with a "micropenis." The women were then asked whether they would have wanted their parents to sanction clitoral surgery, and the men were asked whether they would elect to stay as male (with an unusually small penis) or to undergo sex reassignment. The overwhelming response from both groups was that they should be "let be." Interestingly, in a second study in which a different group of students was asked to imagine that their child was born with ambiguous genitalia, most said they would consent to surgical modification. So why, asks Feder, might people be inclined to make one choice about their own bodies and a significantly different decision about their children's bodies? And further, whose "best interests" are served by these seemingly disparate responses (189–90)?

The implication of Feder's essay is that such decisions are less the result of conscious, rational, and intentional processes than of habitus in Bourdieu's terms as both a structured structure and a structuring structure, which tends to confirm and reinforce dominant modes of perception. Habitus functions, writes Bourdieu, as "durable dispositions." In other words, the notion of habitus makes visible "a kind of implicit normative order . . . that nowhere spells out the rules, that nowhere commands obedience to rules, but works, at the same time, to regulate practices in conformity with a prevailing social order."[17] We clearly see this at work in the current disparity between the legal status of so-called female genital mutilation and what Cheryl Chase refers to as "intersex genital mutilation."[18] These "cultural conventions" of which Bourdieu speaks are not consciously enacted after rational consideration on the part of the individual but work *through* individuals at the level of sensibility. This notion of habitus, then—of "embodied dispositions . . . inculcated from infancy on"—may help explain why medical practitioners often perceive as mutilatory what could be regarded as sex differentiation surgeries performed in non-Western cultures, while intersex surgeries are perceived as therapeutic and necessary.[19] It is not that the reasoning of medical practitioners is simply faulty, but that their habitus structures their perception of "female genital mutilation" and intersex genital modification(s) prior to any rational consideration.

Feder's exegesis of Bourdieu's notion of habitus provides a way to understand what one might perceive as conformity to "the imperative of normality" that moves beyond the idea that parents who consent to normalizing surgeries on behalf of their children are either cultural dupes or self-interested monsters. Feder concludes her article, however, with the seemingly contradictory suggestion that parents "need to work to identify with their children as intersexed individuals," thereby recognizing that "the current management of intersex is a function of habitus" and "work[ing] against the conservative principles of habitus to effect social change."[20] While I agree with Feder that change is both possible and desirable, it cannot simply be effected—as Feder's own account of habitus clearly demonstrates—by identifying the operation of habitus in particular external institutions and practices such as those associated with medicine. This presumes that in doing so we can consciously and intentionally transcend such operations or turn away from them: yet as Feder following Bourdieu notes, habitus works *through* individuals. What perhaps needs to be added to this insight is that in working through us, habitus constitutes us as particular kinds of individuals, it *situates* us in context specific—albeit multiple, complex, and contradictory—ways relative to particular embodied conditions, others, and a world. So, for example, the epistemological ground of parenthood, my dwelling, situates me such that I am not my child: I am not in his/her (embodied) (dis)position, nor can I be. I can only imagine/perceive his/her situation, and my imagining/perception will inevitably be (in)formed by my (dis)position, my dwelling, as "parent."[21] The point is that as a parent I inevitably perceive my child *not* as self but as my child, as the person it is my responsibility to nurture, protect, and so on, in ways that are intelligible (and here intelligibility is "sensible"), in ways that "feel right" and are in keeping not with the knowledge I *have* but with the knowledge I *am*. Such knowledge is evoked mimetically, not consciously, and thereby works *through* me at the most visceral level.[22] It is not that I am first a parent and then I behave in ways appropriate (or otherwise) to my (biological) position; rather, my (dis)position as a parent is "constituted through the repetition of practices or bodily acts the character of which is governed by the habitat I occupy."[23] As Sara Ruddick has demonstrated at length, "caring for children is a *practice* — that is, a socially recognized set of behaviors that is governed by rules and has a point": I inhabit this practice and it inhabits me.[24]

This suggests that while one is never reducible to an other, one is never entirely separate from others either, and consequently particular kinds of (social) relations come to matter in ways specific to one's habitat, the context in which one dwells intercorporeally. As the contributions to *Surgically Shaping Children* by Aspinall, Lisa Abelow Hedley, Eva Feder Kittay, Sherri G. Morris, and Emily Sullivan Sanford in particular demonstrate, child-parent relations as they are constituted and lived in the contemporary West entail a necessarily conflicted symbiosis: as Luce Irigaray so eloquently puts it, "one does not stir without the other."[25] This being the case, the question of whose best interests are served by particular decisions and decision-making practices — a question raised by many of the essays in the three collections under review — is both an impossible and a necessary one. Indeed, what all three collections make clear (in both their titles and contents) is that what is at stake here is not simply a question of ethics, but more precisely *the* question of ethics.

Drawing attention to the fact that the term *ethics* derives from the Greek word *ethos*, meaning character and dwelling, or habitat, Rosalyn Diprose argues that "ethics can be defined as the study and practice of that which constitutes one's embodied habitat, or as the problematic of the constitution of one's embodied place in the world."[26] She further notes that "an ethics based on the problematic of place[ing] . . . claims that our 'being' and the 'world' are constituted by the relation 'in.'" Unlike the notion of ethics as the practice of establishing universal moral principles, this understanding of ethics "recognizes a [mutually] constitutive relation between one's world (habitat) and one's embodied character (ethos)" (19). It is informed by an understanding of bodies (of flesh, of knowledge, of the socius) as always already situated. To appropriate a phrase from Donna Haraway, this conception of ethics — one glimpsed only fleetingly in the collections here discussed — refutes the view from nowhere/everywhere, embracing instead the idea that locatedness "is the condition of articulation, embodiment, and mor[(]t[)]ality."[27]

A number of the essays in both *Surgically Shaping Children* and *Ethics and Intersex* explicitly tackle at length the question of how one might ensure that the treatment of atypical infant bodies is in their best interests, that it is ethical. For example, in an article titled "International Legal Developments Protecting the Autonomy Rights of Sexual Minorities: Who Should Determine the Appropriate Treatment for an Intersex Infant?" Julie A. Greenberg discusses the Constitutional Court of Colombia's compromise decision to allow parents to continue to consent to surgeries on the proviso that parental consent is based solely on the child's best interests and not on parental self-interest.[28] To guarantee that the child's interests are the only (or at least the primary) concern, it was decided by the Court that consent must be in writing, that parents must be provided with a full range of paradigms for understanding and responding to their child's "condition," and that authorization be given on several occasions over an extended period of time, rather than in the emotionally charged situation immediately following the "discovery" of the "condition."

While such safeguards may at first glance seem straightforward, the difficulty in deciding what exactly are the child's best interests, and then clearly distinguishing these from the interests of parents, as well as from the cultural context in which both child and parents dwell, is nicely illustrated in a legal case discussed by Sytsma in a chapter titled "Intersexuality, Cultural Influences, and Cultural Relativism."[29] The case, which Sytsma uses to argue that cultural disparities regarding the somatechnologies of intersexuality should not be resolved by giving precedence to the principle of cultural relativism, involved a thirteen-year-old child from an unnamed Middle Eastern country, who had been brought by his parents to a hospital in the United States during a short vacation. The child had obvious breast development (for which he had been teased by peers) and hypospadias and had experienced unexplained bleeding through the penis. Tests revealed that the child had a 46XX karotype, ovaries, a partial uterus, and congenital adrenal hyperplasia (CAH). The child had been raised as a boy and, as Sytsma somewhat puzzlingly puts it, "manifested a propensity toward masculine gender behavior, although he was unusually fond of children" (260). The parents requested that the child's masculine gender identity be retained and that his body be modified to reflect this (through hypospadias repair, ongoing hormone treatment, and the removal of the ovaries, uterus, and breasts, thereby sacrificing the child's female procreative capacity). They requested that he not be informed of his condition but be told that he was simply undergoing a kidney replacement, which was also necessary and could be performed at the same time. The parents argued that this would be in the child's best interests, since they came from a culture in which the male sex is preferred, only males have rights, and homosexuality is regarded as aberrant. This request presented a problem for the medical team, who felt that the child should be informed and should be an active participant in the decisions about his body, his identity, his reproductive capacity, his future. Clearly the medical team's (dis)position was informed by the relatively recent move in the United States and other Western nations toward full disclosure.

The medical team had other concerns, including the fact that in the United States neonates with CAH have traditionally been assigned female to maintain potential reproductive capacity. In short, the team members felt that the parents' interests were overriding what they perceived as the best interests of the child. The parents, on the other hand, argued that they were making a case based on what they understood as the best interests of the child (interests that could not be divorced from, and were specific to, the cultural context in which the child dwelt — a cultural context significantly different from the one that informed the perceptions of the medical team).[30] So what should be done in a situation in which one party believes a particular decision is in the child's best interests, and another party believes that it is not?

Dreger's response to this question is to invoke the notion of universal rights (and, by association, universal wrongs) with reference to female circumcision.[31] In her contribution to *Ethics and Intersex* Dreger recounts two anecdotes in support of her call for a "re-thinking [of] infant genital cosmetic surgeries as a human (rights) issue."[32] The first — and the one that most interests me — involves a conversation between Dreger and a prominent intersex surgeon in which Dreger poses the question of whether the surgeon — who holds the opinion that "you have to do what parents want" — would be willing to fulfill a request by African parents to alter their daughter's genitalia surgically in accordance with vulval norms specific to their culture. The surgeon says that he would not, since "it would be wrong to cut her for this reason," and justifies his (seemingly contradictory) position by explaining that the difference between female circumcision and surgical sex assignment is that the former constitutes the mutilation of normal genitalia, whereas the latter corrects abnormal genitalia (79).[33] As one would expect, Dreger challenges this distinction, but she does so not by mounting a critique of the historically and culturally specific character of normalcy and pathology — something Eva Feder Kittay tackles at length in her contribution to *Surgically Shaping Children* — but by proclaiming the humanness of the (intersex) child and the universality of the child's rights. She writes, "If we consider the African girl's genital integrity as a matter of human (universal) rights, then the only way to cut the intersex girl's genitals for social reasons is to exempt her from human rights—i.e., to declare her non-human, sub-human or pre-human" (79). For Dreger, then, "intersex is about being a human being, and . . . therefore ethical analyses of intersex should focus on what it means to treat a patient as a full-fledged member of the human race" (81).

Clearly, Dreger's argument presupposes a notion of "the human" that is at once universal, essential, definable, and sacrosanct. Such a notion of the human lies at the very heart of human rights and of human rights law that aims to protect what is (allegedly) innately valuable about human life and its situation within a universal order. Integral to the logic of human rights is the idea that particular things are universally right or wrong. Drawing on this logic, Dreger argues that "*it's just wrong to cut healthy tissue off a girl's clitoris unless she herself wants it cut off and she knows the risks*" (81; emphasis in original).[34] Likewise, in a response to the aforementioned case discussed by Sytsma, Dreger and coauthor Bruce Wilson argue that human rights should take precedence over cultural relativism, stating that "there is no compelling reason to override the right to self-determination of this child, and there are many reasons not to override it. Some might argue that the cultural differences justify following the father's wishes. Nevertheless, we are unsympathetic to the idea that sexual anatomies are an accepted locale for cultural relativism."[35]

While I empathize with the attempts made by many of the contributors to the collections edited by Dreger and Sytsma to argue for a moratorium on "medically unnecessary" infant sex reassignment, I am nevertheless troubled by the increasing dependence on the language and logic of human rights, which not only relies on and reiterates what poststructuralist theorists such as Judith Butler, Jacques Derrida, and Michel Foucault have demonstrated to be a problematic notion of the human subject, but ironically reproduces the very intolerance to difference that Dreger and many of her colleagues set out to challenge. Nowhere is this more apparent that in Sytsma's response to the aforementioned case, in which she states that

> respecting other cultures does not . . . imply that all cultural norms and practices are morally permissible. Recognizing the duty to respect other cultures does not commit one to the acceptance of cultural relativism—the view that actions are right or wrong only in reference to their coherence or incoherence with prevailing cultural values. Resolving or managing cultural conflicts requires impartiality, careful balancing, and discernment. . . .

> Just as when differences exist in morals on a personal level, it is better to
> explain, provide reasons, and demonstrate (where possible) the superiority
> of our own views, it is better to encourage change from within the culture
> than to impose it from without, because values forcefully imposed are not
> authentically held, and relapse is likely to occur. If the differences are
> severe, the best response might be a parting of ways, either on the personal
> or the cultural level. On the cultural level the parting of ways could consist
> in a decision to boycott or to refuse opportunity for commercial trade.[36]

Sytsma's position brings to light the many dangers involved in presuming one's
own "construction of self to be the ideal or 'natural' human state."[37] In dismissing
"cultural relativism" by implying that ultimately one view is the correct one (even
if it does require explanation), that there is a "common good," one inevitably —
and indeed ironically, given that this is the logic that invests medicine/science
with authority over subjugated knowledges — fails to interrogate critically the situ-
atedness, constructedness, and partiality of one's own (dis)position, and perhaps
more troubling still of the ethico-political effects of such on others. One fails to
consider that, as Diprose puts it,

> the regimes of social regulation, which dictate the right way to live, implic-
> itly or explicitly seek to preserve the integrity of every body such that
> we are compatible with the social body. Not only do these thereby dic-
> tate which embodied existences can be transformed by whom and to what
> end, but, as it is here that comparisons are made and values born, not all
> bodies are counted as socially viable. In short, the privilege of a stable
> place within that social and political place we call the "common good" is
> secured at the cost of denigrating and excluding others.[38]

While those authors who take a human rights and/or universalist position
also seem to imply an original (ideal) anatomy, an unmediated form of genitalia
that is opposed to that which has been mutilated, other contributors to the collections under review clearly illustrate the complex ways in which particular bodies
come to matter and are shaped, not only by medicine but also by somatechnologies
that range from the epistemic to the aesthetic, from the practical to the playful,
and which in fact include human rights discourse. For Hedley, for example, there
is no body that is "natural" or right, just as there is no single, simple answer to
the question of whether or not as parents she and her husband should consent to
certain surgeries on her seven-year-old daughter, LilyClaire, who was diagnosed
at birth with achondroplasia. "For parents like me," she writes, "when it comes

to surgical fixes, all you can be sure of is doubt."³⁹ This insight, combined with the refusal to be paralyzed by an absence of certainty or truth, exemplifies what Morland describes as the ethics of intersex, which "in this historical postmodern moment, begin when we no longer rush to pronounce the single right way to manage intersex, but admit uncertainty, replace dogma with discussion. . . . the ethical way to treat intersexed individuals is to preserve, rather than to surgically abolish, the uncertainties that their bodies provoke."⁴⁰ To this, one might add that one of the most effective ways of keeping debate open and uncertainty alive is by remembering, as Parens's collection does, that questions about surgical modification are, in Priscilla Alderson's words, necessarily "set within questions and assumptions about all other forms of shaping and socializing" subjects.⁴¹ At the same time, the questions raised in relation to particular embodied practices conceived as modificatory/mutilatory are shaped—made possible even—by the habitus, and this too needs to be addressed if we are to give serious consideration to the ethics of intersexuality.

Notes

1. John Jordan, "The Rhetorical Limits of the 'Plastic Body,'" *Quarterly Journal of Speech* 90 (2004): 327–58.
2. Cited in Jordan, "Rhetorical Limits," 333.
3. Anna Munster, "Is There Postlife after Postfeminism? Tropes of Technics and Life in Cyberfeminism," *Australian Feminist Studies* 14 (1999): 121.
4. Lily Kay, *Who Wrote the Book of Life? A History of the Genetic Code* (Stanford: Stanford University Press, 2000), 36.
5. Alice Domurat Dreger, "A History of Intersex: From the Age of Gonads to the Age of Consent," in *Intersex in the Age of Ethics*, ed. Alice Domurat Dreger (Hagerstown, MD: University Publishing Group, 1999), 13; Michel Foucault, *"Society Must Be Defended": Lectures at the Collège de France, 1975–76*, ed. Mauro Bertani and Alessandro Fontana, trans. David Macey (London: Penguin, 2004), 7.
6. Alice Domurat Dreger, *Hermaphrodites and the Medical Invention of Sex* (Cambridge, MA: Harvard University Press, 1998), 170.
7. Dreger, *Hermaphrodites*, 170–73.
8. Alice Domurat Dreger, "Intersex and Human Rights: The Long View," in *Ethics and Intersex*, ed. Sharon E. Sytsma (Dordrecht: Springer, 2006), 73.
9. Sharon E. Sytsma, introduction to Sytsma, *Ethics and Intersex*, xix.
10. Iain Morland, "Postmodern Intersex," in Sytsma, *Ethics and Intersex*, 303.
11. See Margrit Shildrick, "Beyond the Body of Bioethics: Challenging the Conventions," in *Ethics of the Body: Postconventional Challenges*, ed. Margrit Shildrick and Roxanne Mykitiuk (Cambridge, MA: MIT Press, 2005), 1–26.

12. Dreger, "Intersex and Human Rights," 75.

13. Erik Parens, introduction to *Surgically Shaping Children: Technology, Ethics, and the Pursuit of Normality*, ed. Erik Parens (Baltimore: Johns Hopkins University Press, 2006), xv.

14. Helena Harmon-Smith, "A Mother's 10 Commandments to Medical Professionals: Treating Intersex in the Newborn," in Dreger, *Intersex in the Age of Ethics*, 195–96; Alice Domurat Dreger and Cheryl Chase, "A Mother's Care: An Interview with 'Sue' and 'Margaret,'" in Dreger, *Intersex in the Age of Ethics*, 83–89; Cassandra Aspinall, "Do I Make You Uncomfortable? Reflections on Using Surgery to Reduce the Distress of Others," in Parens, *Surgically Shaping Children*, 13–28; Lisa Abelow Hedley, "The Seduction of the Surgical Fix," in Parens, *Surgically Shaping Children*, 43–48; Eva Feder Kittay, "Thoughts on the Desire for Normality," in Parens, *Surgically Shaping Children*, 90–110.

15. Dreger, "Intersex and Human Rights," 74.

16. Ellen K. Feder, "'In Their Best Interests': Parents' Experience of Atypical Genitalia," in Parens, *Surgically Shaping Children*, 190.

17. Bourdieu cited in Feder, "Best Interests," 191.

18. Cheryl Chase, "Hermaphrodites with Attitude: Mapping the Emergence of Intersex Political Activism," *GLQ* 4 (1998): 204.

19. Janice Boddy, "Violence Embodied? Circumcision, Gender Politics, and Cultural Aesthetics," in *Rethinking Violence against Women*, ed. R. Emerson Dobash and Russell P. Dobash (London: Sage, 1998), 99.

20. Feder, "Best Interests," 206.

21. Bordieu suggests that habitus adjusts itself to a probable future that it anticipates in the present and thereby helps bring about (cited in Feder, "Best Interests," 205). So one's perception of the future of one's child is necessarily shaped by the knowledge that informs one's bodily (dis)positions in the present.

22. See Boddy, "Violence Embodied?" 105.

23. Rosalyn Diprose, *The Bodies of Women: Ethics, Embodiment, and Sexual Difference* (New York: Routledge, 1994), 19.

24. Cited in Hilde Lindemann, "The Power of Parents and the Agency of Children," in Parens, *Surgically Shaping Children*, 176.

25. Aspinall, "Do I Make You Uncomfortable?"; Hedley, "Seduction of the Surgical Fix"; Kittay, "Thoughts on the Desire"; Sherri G. Morris, "Twisted Lies: My Journey in an Imperfect Body," in Parens, *Surgically Shaping Children*, 3–12; Emily Sullivan Sanford, "My Shoe Size Stayed the Same: Maintaining a Positive Sense of Identity with Achondroplasia and Limb-Lengthening Surgeries," in Parens, *Surgically Shaping Children*, 29–42; Luce Irigaray, "And One Does Not Stir without the Other," *Signs* 7 (1981): 60–67.

26. Diprose, *Bodies of Women*, 19.

27. Donna Haraway, *Modest_Witness@Second_Millennium.FemaleMan©_Meets_ Onco Mouse™: Feminism and Technoscience* (New York: Routledge, 1997), 37.

28. Julie A. Greenberg, "International Legal Developments Protecting the Autonomy Rights of Sexual Minorities: Who Should Determine the Appropriate Treatment for an Intersex Infant?" in Sytsma, *Ethics and Intersex*, 87–102.

29. Sharon E. Sytsma, "Intersexuality, Cultural Influences, and Cultural Relativism," in Sytsma, *Ethics and Intersex*, 259–70.

30. This situation shows that attitudes toward intersexuality (and the somatechnologies of which "intersexuality" as a medicalized condition is an effect) "are clearly tied to cultural values" (Sytsma, "Intersexuality," 262). Such a claim is further supported by the fact that, as Sytsma notes, "in cultures that accord preference to the male gender, there are more sex assignments to the male gender, just as there are fewer cases of male infanticide or abortion of male fetuses" (262). Warne and Bhatia's contribution to *Ethics and Intersex* elaborates more fully on the cultural specificity of intersex treatment (Garry Warne and Vijayalakshmi Bhatia, "Intersex, East and West," in Sytsma, *Ethics and Intersex*, 183–206).

31. Also referred to as "female genital cutting," "female genital practices," or "female genital mutilation."

32. Dreger, "Intersex and Human Rights," 79.

33. In a critique of dominant Western understandings of intersex surgery and so-called FGM, Cheryl Chase notes her concern that "their" genital cutting is depicted as barbaric, whereas "ours" is represented as scientific ("'Cultural Practice' or 'Reconstructive Surgery'? U.S. Genital Cutting, the Intersex Movement, and Medical Double Standards," in *Genital Cutting and Transnational Sisterhood*, ed. Stanlie M. James and Claire C. Robertson [Chicago: University of Illinois Press, 2002], 142–43).

34. Similarly, in a critique that relies on and reproduces the human rights justification used by (some) Western nations to criminalize FGM, Chase writes: "African mothers, no less than American surgeons, act from a desire to care for their daughters. American surgeons, no less than African mothers, are misguided when they direct a knife at a child's clitoris" ("Surgical Progress Is Not the Answer to Intersexuality," in Dreger, *Intersex in the Age of Ethics*, 152).

35. Alice Dreger and Bruce Wilson, "Culture Clash Involving Intersex: Commentary," *Hastings Center Report* 33, no. 4 (2003): 14.

36. Sytsma, "Intersexuality," 264.

37. Boddy, "Violence Embodied?" 95.

38. Diprose, *Bodies of Women*, 131.

39. Hedley, "Seduction of the Surgical Fix," 48.

40. Morland, "Postmodern Intersex," 331.

41. Priscilla Alderson, "Who Should Decide and How?" in Parens, *Surgically Shaping Children*, 167.

THE USES OF ABJECTION

David Kurnick

What Do Gay Men Want? An Essay on Sex, Risk, and Subjectivity
David Halperin
Ann Arbor: University of Michigan Press, 2007. 167 pp.

Risk, the word anchoring the subtitle of David Halperin's frequently profound and occasionally baffling new book, has at least two meanings. Explicitly, Halperin is talking about sexual risk, prompted by evidence of rising HIV infection rates among men who have sex with men. Halperin chooses, provocatively, to begin making sense of these statistics by delving into the "distinctive properties of queer subjectivity" (4)—and the risk that often feels most threatening here is the one queer critics run in talking about gay subjectivity at all. Halperin is acutely aware of how the accident of AIDS gave a grim energy to the association of the queer psyche with morbidity. Wary of colluding with such logics, Halperin makes clear that he is not presenting the truth of the gay subject; he is particularly eager to avoid "the presumptively objective, theoretically elaborated, scientific languages of psychology and psychoanalysis" (104). The book culminates by proposing abjection as a model for a sociohistorically sensitive account of queer subjectivity. Conscious that abjection is hardly devoid of psychic implications, Halperin offers a number of adjectives—"aesthetic" (82), "existential" (103), "ethical" (57), "social" (71), "phenomenological" (104)—to distinguish his approach from psychoanalytic ones. The imprecision here is the point: Halperin combines discrete conceptual lexicons to resist the authority of any vocabulary in particular.

The book opens with a meticulously documented analysis of gay men's sexual risk taking. The figures Halperin marshals demonstrate how infrequently condomless sex between men testifies to some ineffable gay will to self-destruction. Halperin argues that what looks to mainstream media like the reckless abandon of "barebacking" figures in other contexts as the prevention tool of "serosorting." Halperin is doubtful about the effectiveness of serosorting—especially when men don't know their status or come to sexual encounters with varying assumptions about what it means when their partners offer to fuck without latex. But he makes it clear that repeating the panicked question "What makes them do it?" is unlikely to help us recognize—and profit from—the self-preservative resources of queer culture. In the book's less successful middle sections Halperin analyzes a 1995 *Village Voice* article in which Michael Warner candidly discussed his own unsafe encounters. Halperin commends Warner for making serious proposals about why gay men take sexual risks but faults him for letting his analysis slip into psychological terminology. But on the evidence of Warner's article (reprinted in an appendix), Halperin misconstrues Warner's tone. Warner remarks that the headiness of unsafe sex made him feel that "[his] monster was in charge," but this description of an unsettling experience doesn't upstage the careful social analysis that follows; when Halperin labels this a "flirtation with gay demonology" (61), the melodrama is his, not Warner's. And Warner's use of concepts like "ambivalence," "identification," and the "unconscious" leads less to Halperin's point about the difficulty of "detach[ing] psychoanalytic reasoning from normative thinking" (60) than to the conclusion that we don't need a purified lexicon to do vitally queer thinking. Halperin has little to say about the current therapeutic reality in the developed world, although he acknowledges that Warner's article was published just before antiretroviral cocktails made HIV manageable for some. But today's reality on the ground, in which the uneven but widespread availability of drug combinations makes the connection between unsafe sex and HIV infection—and between HIV infection and illness—harder to assume, is surely a factor in assessing how men understand sexual risk.

The most powerful part of the book is an excavation of the concept of abjection in the work of Jean Genet. Halperin describes abjection as an "involuntary, inverted sainthood" (73)—a process in which outcasts defiantly revel in the terms of their social exclusion and find a modicum of safety and power in their collective freedom from acceptance. Halperin offers attentive analyses of two exhilarating and weird scenes of humiliation in Genet's work (including one involving a tube of mentholated vaseline). His readings trace an alchemy of mortification into joy that seems at once peculiar to Genet and instantly recognizable as a widespread affect of queer solidarity. Abjection, Halperin argues, accounts for "generalized effects of social oppression" without turning to individualizing accounts of "unique psychic damage" (76), and it emerges convincingly here as "an existential survival strategy" (72). The reading culminates in the speculative suggestion that gay men's sexual risk taking may be "a scary but inspired expression of antisocial solidarity with their sick or dead comrades in ignominy" (90). The use of this possibility for HIV prevention strategies, Halperin acknowledges, may be hard to see (especially among men who may not understand themselves as gay in the first place, let alone understand risk as an expression of comradeship). Still, Halperin's observation that abjection can conceptually "de-dramatize the practice of sexual risk" (96) is valuable and provocative.

These insights are formulated under the very real pressure of a moment when every twist in the epidemic invites popular speculation about what is wrong with gay men. But Halperin seems to perceive the urge to psychologize as emanating equally from within queer theory. He claims to write "against the intellectual monoculture of psychology" (105), but the only psychoanalytic critic he regularly quotes is Tim Dean. Halperin argues persuasively against Dean's recourse to the death drive as an explanation for gay men's risk taking. But the existence of Dean's work hardly justifies the suggestion that psychoanalysis is close to becoming "the only show in homo-town" (98). Moreover, Halperin's sympathetic engagement with the work of Warner, Douglas Crimp, Didier Eribon, Leo Bersani, Lauren Berlant, and Michel Foucault (not exactly small fry) sits oddly with the embattled tone of much of his book. *What Do Gay Men Want?* is not nearly as lonely in its commitments as Halperin appears to believe. He sometimes writes as if this book, with its refusal to pathologize queerness, its determination to find sociohistorical explanations for queer behavior, and its passionate investment in collective forms of queer existence, inhabits the outer margins of queer theory; I would place it instead in its best tradition.

David Kurnick is assistant professor of English at Rutgers University.

DOI 10.1215/10642684-2008-141

TRANSPARENT FIGURES

Michael D. Snediker

Feeling Backward: Loss and the Politics of Queer History
Heather Love
Cambridge, MA: Harvard University Press, 2007. 206 pp.

*H*eather Love's *Feeling Backward* contributes a perspicuous and often elo-
quent set of literary analyses to the ever-fomenting discourse of queer negativity.
Love's study complicates (rather than reconsolidates or differently hypostasizes)
a possible politics of negative feeling, in part to the extent that its theoretical
vocabulary adheres to (rather than anticipates) the particularities of the authors at
hand. Through readings of Walter Pater, Willa Cather, Radclyffe Hall, and Sylvia
Townsend Warner, Love argues for a politics capable of preserving and learning
from the contretemps that make such a politics necessary in the first place.

     Feeling Backward arises from Love's troubled sense that queer studies
has inoculated or alchemized an archive of negativity, thereby emptying that past,
that "queer history," of the negative qualities by which it was constituted. Despite
the dexterity of Love's local arguments, the specific occasion for Love's intervention feels less persuasive, more familiar. The book's opening gambit is to claim
that "many contemporary critics dismiss negative or dark representations entirely,
arguing that the depiction of same-sex love as impossible, tragic, and doomed to
failure is purely ideological" (1). *Feeling Backward* is peppered with formulations
such as "contemporary critics," "recent critics," "a long [critical] tradition," but
when it comes to those critics and participants of queer studies who imagine "utopian desires . . . at the heart of the collective project of queer studies and integral
to the history of gay and lesbian identity" (3), these critics go unnamed. Does it go
without saying that we know who these critics are?

     Love is not alone in conjuring this spectral queer "utopian" critic (I think,
for instance, of the work of Ann Cvetkovich, Lee Edelman, and David Eng, whom
Love cites as influences). But Love's readings are strong enough on their own not
to require the straw figure of a sort of criticism that doesn't (as far as I'm concerned) so self-explanatorily exist. This is to say that *Feeling Backward* feels most
persuasive as a complication of negativity's own terrain rather than as an interven-

tion in the mirage of utopian queer thinking—which may at most be analogous but by no means equivalent to an "upgrade in gay, lesbian, and transgender life in the United States during the last couple of decades" (189).

The pas de deux between thought and action—texts and lives—recurrently strikes me as one of this study's most interestingly undertheorized sites. It is interesting, as opposed to debilitating, insofar as this dance is *Feeling Backward*'s theoretical and methodological heart. How to learn from the relationships between characters (or authors and characters, or authors and readers, etc.)? How to move from the rhetorical to the ontological when Love seeks even in the moment of movement to recalibrate the terms and conditions of both categories?

Sometimes, as in her tendency to describe her book's terrain as modernism's "dark side" (4)—a formulation that conjures a queer Darth Vader (as though Darth Vader weren't already queer)—Love admits that her archive of negativity is ineluctably, rhetorically imbued. Love likewise telegraphically suggests that feeling backward is itself a "figure of figuration" (5). Other times, however—as in her claim that "sometimes damage is just damage" (27)—*Feeling Backward* intimates a preference for the nonrhetorically tautological over the rhetorically transformative. What does it mean for damage to be "just damage"?

That a referent and its referend could "just" align themselves with each other overlooks the extent to which these readings are predicated on "figures of figuration." If we are speaking of loss at the level of text (which seems safe enough a guess, given the book's literary provenance), then the slippage or nonslippage of referents *does* seem a pertinent issue. *Feeling Backward* tries to have it both ways (figure of figuration/damage = damage) by positing "figures of backwardness as allegories of queer historical experience" (5). Without, however, a keener sense of figuration (not to mention allegory), I am left wishing for more explicit an account of the interstices and avenues between one side of any given equation (allegories) and the other ("queer historical experience").

For instance: Love offers a thoughtful analysis of Pater's first essay, "Diaphaneitè," and exhorts the possibility of heuristically culling from Pater's nonphenomenology of diaphanousness a model of politics founded on revaluations of withdrawal (rather than activism as conventionally understood). That the movement from textual exemplar to lived model is in fact *non*-diaphanous suggestively arises in Pater's *own* text. Rather than inhabit this particular textual nontransparency, however, Love's reading overlooks what is *not* transparent, thereby missing an opportunity by which her own vocabulary of a politics (or poetics) of the shrinking figure might be honed. Love cites these lines from Pater's essay: "Over and over again the world has been surprised by the heroism, the insight, the passion of this clear crystal nature. Poetry and poetical history have dreamed of a crisis, where it must needs be that some human victim be sent down into the grave. These are they whom in its profound emotion humanity might choose to send" (61). Love continues: "Pater's crystal character is defined not only by his transparency but also by his status as victim. Heroism, insight, and passion are here all bound up in an experience of martyrdom, even scapegoating, as this figure is sent to the grave by all of humanity" (61). This figure however is *not*—at least in Pater's writing—sent to the grave. He *might be*. The disappearance in Love's reading of Pater's subjunctive (its own form of figurative shrinking) echoes the disappearance in Love of the crisis's actual scene: not only a dream but the dream of poetry and poetical history.

How is a dream of crisis different from a crisis? How is a person's dream different from poetry's dream? *Feeling Backward* importantly challenges the nontransparency of negativity. As helpfully, Love's book asks of its readers how we might further think about the nontransparency of figuration—and the nontransparency of a straw figure's own suspicious diaphanousness.

Michael D. Snediker is assistant professor of English at Queen's University.

DOI 10.1215/10642684-2008-142

OF LESBIANS AND TECHNOSPERM

Laura Briggs

Queering Reproduction: Achieving Pregnancy
in the Age of Technoscience
Laura Mamo
Durham, NC: Duke University Press, 2007. xi + 304 pp.

In Queering Reproduction, Laura Mamo invites us to think about the place where "sex with reproduction meets reproduction without sex" (23) in lesbian biotechnological reproduction—donor insemination and IVF. It's a set of questions that, for better or worse, has a huge influence on lesbian life and has interestingly different histories for lesbians and gay men. For both these reasons this is an important book. Mamo steers a course between two compelling earlier arguments—Kath Weston's, that in their chosen-ness, queer families are rewriting the script of kinship, and Ellen Lewin's, that lesbians, in becoming mothers, become more fully women—normalized and mainstreamed.[1] Mamo enters the fray by saying, well, both: lesbian bioreproduction is a hybrid social process, one that both queers the family and draws lesbians into alliance with the heteronormative, state-sanctioned nuclear family.

The book begins with a wonderfully textured recent history of lesbian reproduction beginning with the decidedly low-tech, inexpensive models of the 1970s and 1980s: turkey basters and a male friend willing to jerk off in your bathroom. Knowledge of how to get pregnant without sex was passed along in the workshops and informal networks of the women's health movement. Fast-forward thirty years, and we find lesbians paying astonishing amounts of money for frozen sperm samples, taking hormones, and visiting the offices of fertility specialists. The Oakland Feminist Health Center is now the Sperm Bank of California.

The heart of the book is its fascinating interviews with lesbians attempting pregnancy. We hear individuals reflecting on their negotiations with their partners (or deciding to go it alone), going to therapy (for self-actualization), and maximizing their financial well-being. They reflect on decision points—moving "up" the interventionist ladder from home to doctor's office, from donor insemination to IVF, from candles and romance to technoscientific rationality. They discuss the decision to quit or to do things (like hormones) they thought they'd never do. Some chose donors from among their own circles and friends of friends; others used sperm banks. In the transition from doing it ourselves to high-tech methods, Mamo argues, we got caught up in a matrix that includes genetic determinism, medicine, capitalism, insurance coverage, and heteronormativity.

Why the change from low-tech to technosperm? The fact that sperm banks opened their doors to lesbians was a big factor, as was the HIV/AIDS epidemic (a problem that, Mamo points out, reprotech in the United States could mitigate but does not: European labs are washing sperm to remove HIV, U.S. labs are not). But the thirty-six lesbians whom Mamo interviewed mostly gave a single answer to the question of why high-tech: unequivocal legal rights to their children. A number of bad court decisions have found donors to be legal fathers, even granting donors' parents ("grandparents") more legal standing than lesbian partners. It's too bad that Mamo didn't follow her informants down this road. Granted, it would have changed the book — from one about biomedicine to one about family law — but her informants persuaded me that this is the real story about how reprotech constitutes lesbians as activists, not soccer moms, or maybe both. If lesbians in the 1970s and 1980s were guerrilla fertility doctors, Mamo's twenty-first-century lesbians are guerrilla lawyers, passing around photocopies of donor agreements, expounding the legal benefits of sperm banks (donors don't have parental rights), citing legal cases. One couple she interviewed even tailored their reproductive strategies to make themselves a test case for the Center for Lesbian Rights, using one partner's egg and the other partner's uterus, to try to get both of them on the birth certificate.

By failing to think rigorously about law, the book gets in trouble. Mamo writes things like, "Because gay and lesbians have never been able to marry legally, their relationships are outside the scope of family law" (113), even as she notes Massachusetts's gay marriage statute three pages later. She writes, "Second-parent adoption is the primary way for lesbian co-parents to secure parenthood for the nonbiological mother" (69), and goes on to lament the unfairness of this, citing fees and the intrusiveness of home studies — without noting that this legal route to parenthood is not possible in the majority of states in the United States. This is a big story to miss in a book on lesbian reproduction, even if she does note in passing, forty-seven pages later, that second-parent adoption is only (fully, reliably) legal in thirteen states. (Despite the unfairness of this, all but the most destitute of us living without second-parent adoption would be more than happy to pay three thousand dollars for the right to authorize medical care for our children, pick them up from school without a note from biomom, or worrying about losing our kids in a breakup or with a partner's death.) Even though all her informants are in California, setting their experience in the context of life in the other thirty-seven states would have strengthened the book. Thinking of the legal process as a subject of contestation and activism also would have helped her avoid the ways the book is already dated—marriage and civil unions are allowing "other mothers" to be registered as "fathers" on birth certificates, and even strong domestic partner statutes, like California's as of 2004, have mooted the question of "second parent" adoption in a number of states.

The book's strength is its smart, rich, and textured understanding of the past and present of lesbian communities' negotiations of reproduction, an account that will seem deeply familiar to some readers and not at all to others. This written account of a largely oral and memory-based narrative is a tremendous resource for students and anyone who has not been inside or in close proximity to urban lesbian communities since the mid-1980s in the United States. While Mamo's book leaves some loose ends, it is surely an invitation to other scholars to pick up where she left off.

Note

1. Kath Weston, *Families We Choose: Lesbians, Gays, Kinship* (New York: Columbia University Press, 1991); Ellen Lewin, *Lesbian Mothers: Accounts of Gender in American Culture* (Ithaca: Cornell University Press, 1993).

Laura Briggs is associate professor and head of the Department of Women's Studies at the University of Arizona.

DOI 10.1215/10642684-2008-143

PROGRESSIVE HAUNTINGS

Elizabeth A. Castelli

*Ghosts of Futures Past: Spiritualism and the Cultural Politics
of Nineteenth-Century America*
Molly McGarry
University of California Press, 2008. xiii + 269pp.

*Ghosts of Futures Past: Spiritualism and the Cultural Politics of Nineteenth-
Century America*, a revision of the author's 1999 New York University dissertation,
takes readers on a remarkable tour of nineteenth- and early-twentieth-century
America's affective and relational engagements, engagements embedded simultaneously in personal spiritual virtuosity and communal commitments to social
reform and transformation. The book is highly original in its conception, reflects
exhaustive archival research, and breaks new ground in its innovative reframing
of the American Spiritualist movement in new and illuminating terms. *Ghosts of
Futures Past* promises to make a significant and lasting contribution to the field
of American religious history and to theoretically inflected work in the history of
religion as a whole.

 Ghosts of Futures Past makes an argument both multilayered and complex:
it situates American Spiritualism, a movement that some might wish to push to
the margins of American religious history as an embarrassing and perhaps even
hysterical aberration, at the critical meeting point of a whole range of concerns
that animated nineteenth-century American politics, culture, and religion. The
movement, at an almost metaphysical level, sought to inaugurate a grand experiment that challenged conventional notions of temporality, linking a seemingly
lost past to a vibrant present and promising future. (One wonders if this openness
with respect to time was not a kind of uncanny echo of the spatial openness that
westward expansion represented in the nineteenth-century American imaginary.)
The technological innovations of the nineteenth century, especially the invention
of the telegraph and photography, became conduits through which Spiritualism
articulated its powers of mediation. Spiritualists sought to resolve the tensions that
seemed to reside in the conflict between an emergent discourse of science and the

long-dominant ideological frame of religion by claiming that their spiritual practice was, in fact, itself a science.

   But the history of Spiritualism is also a history of sentiments, and as
McGarry so eloquently argues, the movement helps us understand how many
nineteenth-century middle-class white Americans sought to deal with the experience of loss and grief by creating a medium for mourning—by creating a place in
their lives for mediums who had the capacity to channel the spirits of the dead. Yet
the history of Spiritualism also reaches out into the culture and politics of its time,
influencing numerous strands of nineteenth-century political and cultural history
with Spiritualists' involvement in everything from reform movements and abolition
to women's suffrage, free love, and advocacy for Native Americans. In McGarry's
retelling of the history of Spiritualism, we encounter a much more nuanced, lay-
ered, subtle portrait that moves far beyond many earlier scholarly explorations.
McGarry shows us the forces of gender, race, sex and sexuality, colonial status,
and technological innovation, all emerging as critical features of a religious movement that crystallized the most pressing issues and concerns of its time.

   By the last chapter, McGarry brings the history of Spiritualism into conversation with the theme that has animated so much recent scholarly discussion
of religion—that is, the category of secularism. The book offers a model for how
theoretically engaged scholarship on a particular exemplar or empirical example
drawn from the history of religion can open up a wide range of deeply compelling
theoretical questions that extend far beyond the historical example itself. *Ghosts of
Futures Past* should end up on the reading lists of every theory and method course
in academic religious studies as an exemplary model for students trying to understand how theory works by supplementing the hard labor involved in any focused
empirical study.

   For readers of *GLQ*, chapter 5 ("Secular Spirits: A Queer Genealogy of
Untimely Sexualities") will perhaps be of most obvious interest. In this chapter,
McGarry explores the interweaving of the history of secularism and the history
of sexuality, tracing the intersections of discourses of difference—both religious
and sexual difference—across a broad terrain of domains from medicine to law
to poetry. If Spiritualists shared with their evangelical neighbors a belief in the
perfectability of social relations, they also shared with utopian visionaries of their
time a commitment to shaking off the constraints of conventional gender and sexuality, opening themselves to the transgression of all sorts of difference. At the level
of social life, these commitments included, for example, an openness to the tenets
of the free love movement. At the level of spiritual experience, they underwrote

a willingness to embrace the receptivity of virtuosic mediums who channeled spirits of all genders. McGarry draws important contrasts in this chapter between the Theosophical movement's affinities with emergent sexological discourses and Spiritualism's more fluid notions of identity.

As compelling as any ghost story, *Ghosts of Futures Past* is also theoretically sophisticated, rich in detail, and beautifully written. In an uncannily mimetic turn, the book manages to bring the shadowy past of Spiritualism alive and, for some readers at least, mobilizes a desire to reach across time to encounter the amazing cast of characters who inhabit McGarry's spiritualist world. If the spiritualists offered their clients emotional consolation, McGarry offers us some intellectual version of the same: an abiding sense that we have come by a valuable deposit of knowledge and have learned things we would never have known had we not encountered the virtuosic gifts of this book's author.

Elizabeth A. Castelli is professor of religion at Barnard College at Columbia University.

DOI 10.1215/10642684-2008-144

SCRIPTING SEX IN THE OTTOMAN MIDDLE EAST

Howard H. Chiang

Producing Desire: Changing Sexual Discourse in the Ottoman Middle East, 1500–1900
Dror Ze'evi
Berkeley: University of California Press, 2006. xv + 223 pp.

*A*nyone attempting to write a history of the history of sexuality will quickly realize that North America and Western Europe remain the central focus of the field's leading theoretical and empirical preoccupations. In the world outside twentieth-century Europe and North America in particular, the existing literature on the history of Middle Eastern sexuality is even more impoverished in comparison with, say, the history of sexuality in East Asia. In *Producing Desire*, Dror Ze'evi has not merely established himself as the Ottoman equivalent of Bret Hinsch on China or Gregory Pflugfelder on Japan.[1] In responding to the theoretical-historiographical implications of Michel Foucault's work more explicitly, what Ze'evi accomplishes is remarkably unique in providing historians of sexuality, working on Western regions or not, a perspective on Ottoman Middle Eastern sexuality and, with that, a golden opportunity to reflect on their existing methodological concerns.[2] In this regard, the book is undoubtedly a timely and even sorely needed intervention.

In adopting a *longue durée* historical approach, the book argues a rather counterintuitive thesis: open discourses of sex were gradually erased over four centuries in the Ottoman Empire, which stretched from North Africa through the Arabic-speaking lands of the Fertile Crescent and into Anatolia. To quote Ze'evi's concluding remark, "By the beginning of the twentieth century . . . a veil of silence had descended on sex in Middle Eastern culture" (170). The sources that Ze'evi draws on include medical treatises, legal texts, the literature on morality debates, dream interpretation manuals, the actual scripts of plays performed in the Ottoman shadow theater, and European and Middle Eastern travelogues. Each source type defines what Ze'evi calls a sexual "script," a concept he borrows from the sociologist John Gagnon and defines as "a metaphor for the internal and external blueprints in our minds for sexual quest and sexual actions" (10). Accordingly, the book is structured around six main chapters, each devoted to a type of sexual script. Middle Eastern historians might find the book's latter half more innovative than the first, partly because the source base in these later chapters offers us fresh angles to view the sexual past of the region and period under consideration.

In analyzing the six different sexual scripts, Ze'evi never loses sight of the theme of homoerotic sex. In the realm of medicine, the multiple systems of Ottoman law, Sufi morality debates over the beauty of beardless boys, and the science of dream interpretation, open discussions of male homoeroticism, and in some instances even female homoeroticism, were gradually silenced by the nineteenth-century onset of the intensification of the European–Middle Eastern cultural encounter. When European travelogues were eventually translated into Turkish and Arabic, for instance, Ottoman writers responded by fashioning "a clear, new, and comprehensive sense of bounded sexuality with a heteronormal center and 'deviant' margins" (168). This strikes a strong resonance with Afsaneh Najmabadi's recent observation of the heteronormalization of love and the feminization of beauty in the modern Persian world.[3]

A key strength of this succinct monograph lies in the author's careful incorporation of sufficient, rather than overwhelming, historical background material. This allows readers not familiar with Ottoman history to appreciate the historical significance of the various sexual scripts under discussion. However, with respect to the conceptual framing of the book, there are two major criticisms. One concerns how Ze'evi employs the analytic concept of script. One wonders, by the end of the book, whether Ze'evi has underspecified its operational definition on the level of historical analysis. Are "sexual scripts," as the term is used throughout the book, simply discursive fields of sexual *representation*? What is "counter" about "counter-script," a term Ze'evi uses to describe the cultural narrative of the shadow theater? Is it "counter" with respect to its mere social function or actual content? This is one area where Ze'evi could have expanded the scope of his analysis, perhaps by engaging with the notion of "queer counterpublics" developed by Michael Warner, especially given that both authors deal at great length with the history and theory of the public sphere.[4]

Another potential problem with the book's framing concerns the historicization of the very concept of sexuality. For instance, as Arnold Davidson has demonstrated, it would be rather anachronistic to use sexuality as a category of historical analysis outside the conceptual space associated with what he calls the "psychiatric style of reasoning" that emerged only in the latter half of the nineteenth century.[5] Therefore, it would be interesting to see how Ze'evi's study speaks to the subsequent substantiations of Foucault's claim rather than Foucault's work alone. Despite this reservation, perhaps this book's biggest problematic as set up by the Foucauldian labyrinth of social constructionism could also be the very cradle of its most original historiographical intervention. Unwinding the veil of silence that descended on sex in Middle Eastern culture, *Producing Desire* is a rare book that opens our eyes to an alternative history of sexuality outside the modern world of Euro-America, and, in doing so, opens up our mind to the possibility of forgiving the discourse for its Foucauldian entanglement.[6]

Notes

1. Bret Hinsch, *Passions of the Cut Sleeve: The Male Homosexual Tradition in China* (Berkeley: University of California Press, 1990); Gregory Pflugfelder, *Cartographies of Desire: Male-Male Sexuality in Japanese Discourse, 1600–1950* (Berkeley: University of California Press, 1999).

2. I am specifically referring to the insights of Michel Foucault, *An Introduction*, vol. 1 of *The History of Sexuality*, trans. Robert Hurley (New York: Vintage, 1990).

3. Afsaneh Najmabadi, *Women with Mustaches and Men without Beards: Gender and Sexual Anxieties of Iranian Modernity* (Berkeley: University of California Press, 2005). See also Khaled El-Rouayheb, *Before Homosexuality in the Arab-Islamic World, 1500–1800* (Chicago: University of Chicago Press, 2006); Joseph Massad, *Desiring Arabs* (Chicago: University of Chicago Press, 2007).

4. Michael Warner, *Publics and Counterpublics* (New York: Zone, 2002).

5. Arnold Davidson, *The Emergence of Sexuality: Historical Epistemology and the Formation of Concepts* (Cambridge, MA: Harvard University Press, 2001).

6. Matt Kuefler, "Forgiving Foucault" (paper presented at the 122nd annual meeting of the American Historical Association, Washington, DC, January 3–6, 2008).

Howard Chiang is a PhD candidate in the Program in History of Science at Princeton University.

DOI 10.1215/10642684-2008-145

HIGH MEDIEVAL ALLEGORY AND COERCION

Anna Klosowska

Allegory and Sexual Ethics in the High Middle Ages
Noah D. Guynn
New York: Palgrave Macmillan, 2007. xii + 218 pp.

*N*oah D. Guynn's new book is a step removed from the history of sexuality: it's a history of discourse. Guynn is well known to all of us in medieval queer studies from his early article on the subject published in *GLQ* in 2000.[1] Other significant articles followed. His first, long-awaited book is not focused on queer studies in the same way, or directly; rather, as the title announces, Guynn shows that "medieval allegory and sexual ethics operate as discursive regimes: they internalize difference, deviation, and dissent within figurations of truth, goodness, and belief, and then use the resulting crisis of meaning, knowledge, and belief to legitimate coercive, violent forms of discipline" (171). A strength of the book is Guynn's command of a wide and exciting range of readings condensed to their essential elements; often, although the names are familiar, the texts are not. Although I disagree with the "Foucauldian" view of history that Guynn adopts, a view where the French Revolution constitutes a paradigm break separating the ancien régime from the emergent modernity, I recognize in his book many of my favorite writers: the philosophers Chantal Mouffe, Louis Althusser, and Giorgio Agamben, as well as U.S. medievalists and early modernists such as Jody Enders and Gordon Teskey, among others.

Guynn's book is clear and forceful, its analyses well observed and written, but I think its omissions mean that the topic (high medieval allegory, specifically in relation to coercion) is too large for one book. To take the first and third chapters, for example (Hugh of Saint-Victor, Saint Augustine, Thomas Aquinas, and Alain de Lille): Guynn's omission of Abelard and Héloïse is important, especially in view of Guynn's sustained interest in women and Aristotle (via Agamben). Abelard's and Héloïse's famous interventions in the twelfth-century debate on meaning (that debate is Guynn's main topic) would modify in essential ways the conclusions that Guynn draws in these chapters. After reading these two chapters, I am not convinced that I grasped the issue of allegory in the High Middle Ages, partly because there is little attempt on Guynn's part to locate geography, history, or intellectual genealogies (for instance, Guynn does not connect the texts he discusses with Boethius's *De consolatione philosophiae*, perhaps the most widely read and taught high medieval allegory). This doesn't make Guynn's book wrong, just more abstract. Moreover, his treatment of Augustine and Aquinas is mainly secondhand, a pity considering how acute and inspiring his readings of *Enéas* and other texts are in this book. One suggestion: a reference to the political situation that produced fourteenth-century French translations of Augustine (a confluence of politics, ideology, and literary activity — precisely the cluster anticipated by Guynn's definition of allegory as a literary device in service of the state and other institutions) would help bridge the period discussed by Guynn (the twelfth and thirteenth centuries) and his isolated example of prosecution of sodomy as a crime against the state (almost sixteenth century), which is out-of-period but essential for his discussion.

Note

1. Noah D. Guynn, "Eternal Flame: State Formation, Deviant Architecture, and the Monumentality of Same-Sex Eroticism in the *Roman d'Enéas*," *GLQ* 6 (2000): 287–319.

Anna Klosowska is associate professor of French at Miami University, Ohio.

DOI 10.1215/10642684-2008-146

SUPERBAD SEX OBJECTS

Jill H. Casid

Sex Objects: Art and the Dialectics of Desire
Jennifer Doyle
Minnesota: University of Minnesota Press, 2006. xxxi + 184 pp.

I remember reading that when "feminism meets queer theory," our encounter begets "more gender trouble."[1] In "Against Proper Objects" (her introduction to that 1994 special issue of *differences*), Judith Butler runs interference in the custodial restriction of gender to women's studies and sex to lesbian and gay studies, to clear the way for a profoundly troubled sense of gender that cannot be cordoned off from sex. A genealogy of queer theory might trace its inception to Teresa de Lauretis's effort to activate feminist theory from within lesbian and gay studies and thereby insist that feminism is already a constitutive part of queer theory. However, the face-offs between women's and lesbian and gay studies continue, particularly over our objects — whether proper or bad.[2] What will it take to get the encounters between feminism and queer theory we deserve?

One answer might be the critical embrace of superbad sex objects that informs Jennifer Doyle's *Sex Objects*. Here contact with those messy, category-defying versions of sex and the ways in which sex "happens in art" is inextricable from our embodiment as feeling and thinking critics, the problematics of capital, and the constructions of race and sexual difference. While Doyle's trafficking in the border zones of feminism and lesbian and gay studies is far from unprecedented, what distinguishes her contribution is in part her transgression of the disciplinary etiquette that would dictate that the proper object of women's and lesbian and gay studies be identity and that we somehow be what we study.

Doyle's critical positioning as a "fag hag" and her extension of her own cross-gender and cross-sexuality friendships to develop the "forms of intimacy that take shape between women (straight and gay) and gay men" (xxv) into not just the object of her work but also its method importantly and productively expand identity-based criticism. This version of the encounter between feminism and queer theory comes close to answering de Lauretis's call that queer theorizing involve the "imaging and enacting of new forms of community by the other-wise desiring subjects of this queer theory."[3] Mobilizing a fag hag optic allows Doyle to bring other "other-wise desiring subjects" and objects into view. Doyle occupies a place within queer theory as one of those "other-wise desiring subjects" whose strong attachments to gay men and elective affinities for homoerotic representations far exceed our Noah's ark taxonomies and transform how we read our desired objects.

In the central chapters of this wide-ranging work, Doyle imaginatively plays the favored hag to Andy Warhol's fag (102). The payoff of this queer feminist perspective is most pronounced in the chapter on women in Warhol's films of the late sixties. In one of the many transhistorical interpretive gestures that distinguish this study, Doyle looks again at these films and the role of women in them from the vantage of the female figure in "the twenty-ninth bather" section of *Leaves of Grass*, whose admiring gaze sets up one of the most explicitly homoerotic scenes in all of Whitman's work (81).[4] Framing our view in this way enables Doyle to argue that because these women are "framed by a gay male context, [they get] to be something other than the straight sex object" (72), and Warhol and Whitman can be seen as protoqueer feminist in their situation of women as those "other-wise desiring subjects."

Like the women in Warhol and Whitman whom Doyle demonstrates to be both "irrelevant, and absolutely central" (71), Doyle activates the minor throughout her readings to demonstrate how the margin is centrally destabilizing to the "proper objects" of American literary and art historical study. The book's provocative preface sets the stage, telling a personally implicating origin story for her formation as a queer feminist critic that links a pornographic photograph of a black man's dick and an L. L. Bean sweater emblazoned with a whale to Herman Melville's *Moby-Dick*, troubling the distinction between ("high") art and ("gay") porn. As the chapters unfold we see the "boring parts," the ancillary figures, and the paratexts fundamentally alter hallowed objects of the canon.

Doyle coedited an anthology of queer readings of Warhol titled *Pop Out*, and it is not just the Yayoi Kusama rowboat fitted up with phallic protrusions which Doyle mobilizes here that makes me want to call this book "Pop Up" to characterize the uncanny effects of reading it.[5] Doyle's relational reading practice stages cross-time, cross-gender and -genre, cross-race, and cross-class encounters between unlikely suspects that also call our attention to the relations between the ways that texts and images hail their readers and to the way Doyle's critical "I" functions as a vehicle for our own. When Doyle writes that "sex happens in art," we are also confronted with the ways that sex, desire, boredom, and pleasure take place between work and reader. The more Doyle writes such passages as

"*Moby-Dick* asks us to take the book off its representational hinges, to touch it as Queequeg touches his book," the more palpable becomes Doyle's own experiment in performing the effects of intimacy, sentimentality, and pornography that she analyzes.

The queer feminist aesthetics of its style appear also in the cheeky, confessional play with academic book structure. In the customary location of a conclusion come the acknowledgments in which we read about Doyle's sisters, the sisters with whom she grew up, and a "larger community of friends" (141). This complicitous solicitation of us as virtual intimates may work to sustain and expand the queer feminist critical community required to continue to give us the encounters of feminism and queer theory we deserve. I do find myself left with some unfulfilled wishes — for example, that the itinerary of Doyle's criticism would take off in the direction of a more transnational version of queer feminist criticism, move beyond black and white, and (though I recognize the incommensurability) stir some ways to be critically smart about not just the fag hag but also the dyke tyke. But prompting such wishes that map where the encounters of feminism and queer theory may go is to be encouraged.

Notes

1. Judith Butler, "Against Proper Objects," *differences* (Summer – Fall 1994): 1–26.
2. Teresa de Lauretis, "Queer Theory: Lesbian and Gay Sexualities, An Introduction," *differences* 3 (Summer 1991): iii–xviii.
3. de Lauretis, "Queer Theory," xvi.
4. Walt Whitman, "Song of Myself," in *Leaves of Grass* (New York: Norton, 2002), sec. 11, ll. 199–216.
5. Jennifer Doyle, Jonathan Flatley, and José Muñoz, *Pop Out: Queer Warhol* (Durham, NC: Duke University Press, 1996).

Jill H. Casid is associate professor of visual culture studies and director of the Visual Culture Center at the University of Wisconsin at Madison.

DOI 10.1215/10642684-2008-147

THE FIGURE OF THE BLACK FEMME AND
HER RADICAL ELSEWHERE

Stacy I. Macías

The Witch's Flight: The Cinematic, the Black Femme,
and the Image of Common Sense
Kara Keeling
Durham, NC: Duke University Press, 2007. ix + 209 pp.

In The Witch's Flight, Kara Keeling seeks to reveal through analyses of black film how cinematic processes structure the experience of our globalized twenty-first-century reality. Keeling focuses on black cinema with a keen eye directed at the rarely seen, just negligible, or violently eclipsed black femme, a spectral figure who—surviving under the yoke of common sense, black cultural nationalism, and cinematic reality—represents a possibility of disrupting the regime of the visual and its hegemonic prescriptions. Set to its own musical soundtrack with firm instructions on when to push play, Keeling's book excavates without compunction from mainstream black cinema an alternative archive of temporality, affect, and ultimately reality. For Keeling, to apprehend an alternative social reality where the processes rationalizing dominant notions of memory, perception, time, labor, race, gender, sexuality, and capital are brought into sharp relief means to find and follow the trajectory of the cinematic presence and absence of the black femme. Along the path of encountering the black femme and all her problematic and sublime offerings, we must also contend with the force of *the cinematic*, "a term through which to shuttle a complicated aggregate of capitalist social relations, sensory-motor arrangements, and cognitive processes" (3).

In the first two chapters, Keeling introduces the elaborate conceptual framework she uses to critique black visual culture. Contextualizing the theoretical insights of Henri Bergson (affect), Gilles Deleuze (the cinematic), Antonio Gramsci (common sense), and Frantz Fanon (temporality), Keeling invents a highly intricate theory to argue that via the cinematic, sensory-motor schema tend to overlay present perception with past images and in so doing achieve familiar recognition in the form of common sense, or cliché, which circumscribes any radically different perception of the future. In other words, when film viewers imbibe a common memory image projected on a screen, the capacity for critical thinking to overcome the power of habituated affect is potentially halted. Imagined futures, alternative becomings, and radical elsewheres consequently dematerialize within the logic of the cinematic and its impulse to advance global capitalism and achieve consent via the facade of redistributive justice. Common sense, however, is never only monolithic or depotentializing; shielded within it are the "seeds of good sense" that "may enable another type of mental and/or motor movement to occur, thereby enabling an alternate perception" (22, 14).

The book's following chapters offer original analysis of how black cinematic productions unwittingly reproduce and inadvertently create hegemonic and counterhegemonic common senses often to the detriment of the black femme figure. Beginning with a consideration of the commonsense black nationalism paramount to Haile Gerima's *Sankofa* (1993), Keeling describes how it relies on a conscientious albeit predictable narrative of slave resistance commensurate with the image of the black male subject, which renders black femininity and the black femme — often indexing black existence to passivity, sexual availability, and inhumanity — a present impossibility. To recall Joon Oluchi Lee's relevant insight, "the specific femme style of a racialized, *black*, girl, like the castrated boy, has its origin in violence."[1]

In chapter 4 I found one of Keeling's most evocative arguments on the (f)utility of black nationalism's masculinity, one that may rattle black feminist theorizations. Black Panther Party members — as "blacks with guns" — appearing on television news and in print media catalyzed an alternative image of the Black who was not inferior but forthrightly armed to break with hegemonic black common sense. Ushered into this visual economy were black women as "blacks with guns," thereby signaling an emergent and radically configured masculinity detached from strict black male inhabitation. As part of the horizon of possibilities for alternative structures of existence, black nationalism's masculinity — before it was habituated — recognized the subjectivity of black women, who had been virulently denied the protection of femininity afforded to pious, pure, and domestic white bourgeois women.

The second half of *The Witch's Flight* considers the blaxploitation films made from 1970 to 1975 and the cable drama *The L Word*; ghettocentricity and lesbian butch-femme in the context of F. Gary Gray's film *Set It Off* (1996); and an encrypted slave past in Kasi Lemmon's *Eve's Bayou* (1997). In this latter portion, the black femme materializes on screen as a vector for nonheteronormativity, as substantiating black female masculinity, and finally as "the black femme function" that "mark[s] a potential for creativity and self-valorization within affectivity that also is useful to the reproduction of cinematic reality" (144).

What Keeling commits to in her critique of black cinema exemplifies one of the book's overall critical values and strengths: it situates historically our contradictory, unconscious desires for calling up the past. For Keeling, the commonsense black nationalism informing black cultural production occurring from the 1960s onward is not only indicative of a minoritized community's response to a vicious history of disenfranchisement beginning with slavery but is a product of the U.S. state's deeply embedded relationship with cinematic reality and its delimiting temporality, where "chronological time posits one true past that has led to one true present that will lead to a true, if indeterminate, future" (77). Like other queer engagements with temporality, *The Witch's Flight* takes seriously the political and cultural implications of nonnormative time for imagining how hidden forms of social relations, knowledges, and systems of becoming fleetingly captured in film can flourish outside it.

Methodologically, *The Witch's Flight* fits squarely on the shelf with other film, visual, and media studies scholarship while also straddling critical U.S. historiography, queer theory, women's studies, and critical race studies. And yet, its methodology represents more than an example of interdisciplinarity precisely because it uniquely embodies a field of thought working to understand its own implication in reproducing global capitalism, neoliberalism, and the ruse of representation.

By Keeling's own admission, *The Witch's Flight* can be cumbersome to manage theoretically and thus will require nonremunerative intellectual labor and attention. Fortunately, we have become so bewitched by the flight of the black femme that the reward is the relentless intellectual acumen with which Keeling carves out an irresistible, alternate future.

Note

1.   Joon Oluchi Lee, "The Joy of the Castrated Boy," *Social Text*, nos. 84–85 (2005): 41.

Stacy I. Macías is a PhD candidate in women's studies at the University of California, Los Angeles.

DOI 10.1215/10642684-2008-148

OF CANINES AND QUEERS

Christopher Peterson

Melancholia's Dog: Reflections on Our Animal Kinship
Alice Kuzniar
Chicago: University of Chicago Press, 2006. x + 215 pp.

In Year of the Dog (dir. Mike White, 2007), a forty-something secretary named Peggy (Molly Shannon) descends into an almost paralyzing state of mourning after the untimely death of her pet dog, Pencil. Refusing to acknowledge the depth of this loss, Peggy's coworker Layla (Regina King) coldly suggests that "maybe your dog died so your love life can live." Obsessed with the rituals of heterosexual courtship and marriage, Layla articulates one of the film's central concerns: the tension between normative, heterosexual love and Peggy's seemingly aberrant love for animals. Layla's concern with her friend's deviant sexuality recalls the hysterical proposition that the legalization of gay marriage will legitimate all sorts of nefarious sexual practices, including bestiality. Yet the film's denouement adopts a sympathetic tenor toward Peggy's decision to reject the heterosexual injunction, abandon her dreary office job, and run off with a new dog to pursue a career as an animal rights activist. The film thus explores how love might live not at the expense of the animal's death but in the form of alternative, interspecies kinship arrangements.

Although not overtly concerned with the politics of queer kinship, Alice Kuzniar's *Melancholia's Dog: Reflections on Our Animal Kinship* poses a number of questions that interrogate the social shame that is often imposed on those who appear inordinately attached to their pets. As Kuzniar observes, "one of the most unutterable aspects of closeness with pets is the shamefulness about intimacy with them, as if it might be construed as bordering on bestiality or as if to love dogs betrayed an inability to love humans" (10). One consequence of this shame, Kuzniar maintains, is the melancholic disavowal of human attachment to animals, a recognition and refusal of the human/animal bond that is exacerbated by the transience of dog lives (compared with human life expectancy): "During the life of pets the propensity is to deny to some degree the intensity of the bond," leading humans bereft of a language to express their grief on the occasion of an animal's death (138). Kuzniar's emphasis on the unspeakable and ungrievable character of dog love intersects with the work of scholars in race, gender, and sexuality studies who have worked to expose the larger cultural violence through which minorities become especially vulnerable to an untimely death.[1] Such an overdetermined affinity with death is compounded, moreover, by the frequent characterization of such deaths as unworthy of grief.[2]

Offering nuanced readings of a wide assortment of literary texts, films, photographs, and paintings by Franz Kafka, J. M. Coetzee, Rebecca Brown, Sally Mann, William Wegman, David Hockney, and Sue Coe (among others), and engaging with a rich panoply of philosophical writings on the human-animal question—Jacques Derrida, Emmanuel Levinas, Sigmund Freud, Ludwig Wittgenstein, and Søren Kierkegaard—Kuzniar offers a compelling and often moving account of human relationships with dogs. For instance, in her reading of *Whym Chow: Flame of Love* (a collection of poems written in 1906 by Katherine Harris Bradley and her niece and lover, Edith Emma Cooper, and published in 1914 under the nom de plume Michael Field), Kuzniar suggests that the authors' expression of grief for their lost dog links "the love that dare not speak its name" to an interspecies love that defies societal norms. In these poems, "sadness is exalted and grief stylized into a worship of the deceased that beatifies the love between the two women" (161). And in her reading of Brown's *The Dogs: A Modern Bestiary*, Kuzniar observes that the narrator's relationship with her dogs "adopts a queer dimension" insofar as its required secrecy (the landlord prohibits pets) mimes the closeting of the narrator's sexuality (130).

While *Melancholia's Dog* displays careful attention to the practices of interspecies grief and mourning, the book's focus on dogs might strike some readers as arbitrary. Kuzniar chooses to interrogate the human-animal divide "precisely via the animal with which the human has the closest contact, namely, the dog" (5). Lovers of cats, fish, horses, snakes, rabbits, and potbellied pigs (the list is necessarily unlimited) would certainly take issue with the assumption that "humans have the most empathetic bond" with dogs (7). This emphasis on proximity, moreover, does not square easily with the book's other emphasis on "the radical alterity of animal being," a theoretical position that Kuzniar adopts from Derrida (18). In her efforts to legitimize and make legible the intimacy and loss that accompany human-dog relationships, Kuzniar does little to challenge the ideal of intimacy itself, and therefore leaves intact its pretensions to nearness and dialectical union. This sublation of alterity is especially evident in her suggestion that estrangement might be understood as fostering intimacy rather than as undoing its fantasy of inwardness and mutual recognition (122). How might our relationship to the "radical alterity" of nonhuman animals contest, instead of simply reaffirm, our normative conceptions of intimacy? What might the alterity of nonhuman animals have to teach us about the alterity of those human animals with whom we imagine the most intimate kinship?

Despite these reservations, *Melancholia's Dog* is a welcome contribution to ongoing discussions on the timely theme of animality, a subject that has produced a wealth of scholarship in recent years at the intersection of literature, philosophy, history, film studies, and cultural theory. Particularly admirable is Kuzniar's bravery in insisting on the relevance of her subject matter, which, as she notes, is often "presumed to be unfit for serious scholarly investigation" (1). Kuzniar demonstrates not only that the topic is worthy of intellectual attention but that its discussion is long overdue.

Notes

1. See Abdul R. JanMohamed, *The Death-Bound-Subject: Richard Wright's Archaeology of Death* (Durham, NC: Duke University Press, 2005); Karla Holloway, *Passed On: African-American Mourning Stories* (Durham, NC: Duke University Press, 2002); Sharon Holland, *Raising the Dead: Readings of Death and (Black) Subjectivity* (Durham, NC: Duke University Press, 2000); Christopher Peterson, *Kindred Specters: Death, Mourning, and American Affinity* (Minneapolis: University of Minnesota Press, 2007).
2. For more on the subject of ungrievable lives, see Judith Butler, *Precarious Life: The Powers of Mourning and Violence* (New York: Verso, 2004).

Christopher Peterson is a lecturer in the School of Humanities and Languages at the University of Western Sydney.

DOI 10.1215/10642684-2008-149

About the Contributors

Sarah M. Creighton is a consultant gynecologist at University College Hospital, London. She is a member of the multidisciplinary team for disorders of sex development (DSD). She has a clinical and research interest in DSD and has published on long-term gynecological and psychosexual sexual outcomes in these conditions.

Alice D. Dreger, PhD, is a Guggenheim fellow, professor of clinical medical humanities and bioethics at the Feinberg School of Medicine of Northwestern University, and the former board chair of the Intersex Society of North America. Her research and advocacy focus on the medical and social treatment of people born with norm-challenging bodies. More information about her work is available through her Web site, www.alicedreger.com.

Ellen K. Feder is associate professor of philosophy at American University. She is author of *Family Bonds: Genealogies of Race and Gender* (2007) and is working on a book on ethics and the medical management of intersex tentatively titled "Disturbing Bodies."

An internationally recognized expert on legal issues relating to gender, sex, sexual identity, and sexual orientation, **Julie A. Greenberg** is professor of law at the Thomas Jefferson School of Law in San Diego. Her work on gender identity has been cited by a number of state and federal courts in the United States as well as courts in other countries. Her book *Sex Matters: Intersexuality and the Law* is forthcoming from NYU Press.

April M. Herndon, PhD, is assistant professor of English and women's and gender studies and director of the WILL Program (Women's Initiative for Learning and Leadership) at Winona State University in Winona, MN. Her research focuses on stigmatized embodiments, and she is especially interested in representations and lived experiences of fatness in contemporary American culture.

Iain Morland is a lecturer in cultural criticism at Cardiff University, where he teaches critical theory, gender studies, and queer theory. He has published widely on the ethics, theory, and psychology of intersex in interdisciplinary journals such as *Textual Practice*, *Continuum*, and *Feminism & Psychology*. He is editor (with Annabelle Willox) of *Queer Theory* (2005).

Katrina Roen is associate professor of societal psychology in the Department of Psychology at the University of Oslo. Her work on gender, sexed embodiment, and psychomedical interventions has emerged out of research on both transsexuality and intersexuality, and draws from queer and poststructuralist feminist approaches. She has also published in *Body and Society, Signs, Journal of Gender Studies*, and *International Journal of Critical Psychology*, among other journals and edited collections.

Vernon A. Rosario is a child psychiatrist and associate clinical professor in the Department of Psychiatry at the University of California, Los Angeles. He is the author of *The Erotic Imagination: French Histories of Perversity* (1997) and *Homosexuality and Science: A Guide to the Debates* (2002). His current clinical research is on sexuality and gender identity in transgender and intersex children and adults.

Nikki Sullivan is associate professor of critical and cultural studies, and director of the Somatechnics Research Centre, at Macquarie University. She is the author of *Tattooed Bodies* (2001), *A Critical Introduction to Queer Theory* (2003), and of numerous articles on forms of body modification.

Del LaGrace Volcano is a visual artist and intersex activist using primarily photography to spread the gender-queer word. His/her pioneering work with sexual and political minorities has helped create a queer and transgender aesthetic and an archive of the sexual micropolitics of the last twenty years. His anthologies include *Love Bites* (1991), *Sublime Mutations* (2000), *The Drag King Book* (with Judith Halberstam, 1999), *Sex Works* (2005), and most recently, *Femmes of Power: Exploding Queer Femininities* (with Ulrika Dahl, 2008). www.dellagracevolcano.com

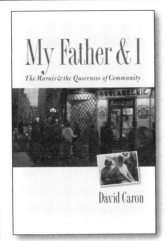